An introduction to the
psychology of religion

# AN INTRODUCTION TO THE
# PSYCHOLOGY OF RELIGION

ROBERT H. THOULESS

*Fellow of Corpus Christi College, Cambridge.*
*Reader Emeritus in Educational Psychology,*
*University of Cambridge*

THIRD EDITION

CAMBRIDGE UNIVERSITY PRESS

*Cambridge*

*London* • *New York* • *Melbourne*

Published by the Syndics of the Cambridge University Press
The Pitt Building, Trumpington Street, Cambridge CB2 1RP
Bentley House, 200 Euston Road, London NW1 2DB
32 East 57th Street, New York, NY 10022, USA
296 Beaconsfield Parade, Middle Park, Melbourne 3206, Australia

First published 1971
Reprinted 1974, 1979

Printed in the United States of America
First printed by Tinling & Co. Ltd., Prescot, Lancs.
Reprinted by LithoCrafters, Inc., Chelsea, Michigan


ISBN 0 521 08149 1 hard covers
ISBN 0 521 09665 0 paperback

# Contents

|  | Preface | *page* vii |
|---|---|---|
| 1. | How the psychological study of religion began | 1 |
| 2. | Psychology and religion | 8 |
| 3. | The psychological roots of religion | 15 |
| 4. | The social factor in religion | 20 |
| 5. | The natural factor in religion | 32 |
| 6. | The moral conflict | 39 |
| 7. | The emotional factor in religion | 48 |
| 8. | Religion and human needs | 58 |
| 9. | The intellectual factor in religion | 65 |
| 10. | Religion and psychotherapy | 73 |
| 11. | Psychical research and religion | 80 |
| 12. | The psychology of prayer | 90 |
| 13. | The psychology of meditation | 96 |
| 14. | The psychology of conversion | 104 |
| 15. | Mysticism | 121 |
| 16. | Practical problems of religious diversity | 132 |
| 17. | The empirical argument for religious faith | 141 |
|  | Index | 149 |

# Preface

The first edition of the present work was published in 1923 under the title *An introduction to the psychology of religion*. It was republished as a paper-back in 1961 without change of text but with a new preface in which I tried to indicate some of the ways in which it would require change if it were revised. Now nearly ten years later, it appears that the book is still being read. Those who are kind enough to want to read it now deserve to have a more up-to-date version, so I have made a radical revision.

The necessity for revision arises primarily from the changes that have taken place during the last half century in psychology and in the methods adopted in the psychological study of religion. Psychology has become increasingly the study of human behaviour and has made use of quantitative methods of enquiry. It is true that Starbuck was already using quantitative methods as early as 1899, but such studies were at first regarded as a somewhat eccentric interest for psychologists and in 1923 I had insufficient appreciation of their importance for the psychological study of religion. The statistical studies in religious psychology which started as a small trickle at the beginning of this century have now become a great river which no-one can ignore. It remains true that the earlier non-quantitative work was of lasting value as a preliminary mapping of the field of enquiry. It not only gives tentative answers to questions which cannot (or cannot yet) be subjected to quantitative enquiry; it also serves the purpose of indicating the points where there arise questions which demand more exact answers than can be given by opinion based on common observation.

I have included in this edition some samples of the kind of quantitative enquiry that has been made. It is not intended to be a comprehensive account of what has been accomplished in this field. That would be the subject matter of a different kind of book that could not be written by me.

There are some special problems in the revision of a book by oneself fifty years ago. There is a temptation to change too much because a man in his seventies is inclined to be intolerant of the rashness and superficiality of a youthful writer, and this intolerance is only a little modified by the consideration that this rash young man was oneself. At the same time, one must recognise that this young man did succeed in writing a book that seems to have interested a succession of readers over a period of nearly fifty years. This is more than his elderly reviser could hope to do himself, and it suggests that revision should not go so far as completely to destroy the character of the original.

I have, therefore, built on the foundations of the old book and largely followed the old chapter headings. Some I have omitted as, for example, the not very illuminating chapter on a modern mystic. Some I have added as, for example, a chapter on psychical research, a topic which should, I think, be included in any modern book on the psychology of religion but about which the original author was almost entirely ignorant. The sixteenth chapter on religious diversity is also wholly new.

While trying to preserve as much as I could of the original structure of the book, I have found it necessary to make much change in detail. Often in the old book I expressed myself in ways I should not now, and I put forward some opinions that I no longer hold. In all such cases I have changed what has been said to what I should say now. In some cases (as in Chapter 17) it has seemed to me that the author expressed himself obscurely and I have tried to express more clearly what he seemed to be trying to say.

In general my aim has been not to suppress the original author but to collaborate with him, in the hope that together we might be able to produce something better than either of us could do separately. I have refrained from cutting out one feature of the original book that is not in line with contemporary literary fashion. We are not now inclined to use illustrative material to the extent that the author did in 1923 (influenced by the example of William James). This feature would probably now be condemned as a tendency to 'anecdotalism'. It has seemed to me, however, that much of the quality of the book depended on this use of illustrative material so I have not tried to cut it out. I have thought, however, that the young author sometimes told his stories at unreasonable length, and have often judged it better to shorten them.

I cannot hope that the original author would have been entirely satisfied with what I have done with his book. He could not, however, have reasonably expected that it would go on being read for nearly half a century. He would, I hope, have appreciated the fact that considerable changes would have become necessary by 1971 if his work were to be expected to last for even a few years beyond that time.

*2, Leys Road*                                     R. H. Thouless
*Cambridge*
*June 1970*

# 1. How the psychological study of religion began

At about the end of the nineteenth century it became apparent that the growing science of psychology provided an instrument for the study of religion, and that such study might serve to increase understanding of religious ways of behaving, thinking, and feeling. It was then that William James, professor at the University of Harvard, was invited to give the Gifford Lectures at Edinburgh University. These lectures, at the four Scottish universities, had been endowed by Lord Gifford to promote the study of religion as a branch of natural science. Many Gifford lecturers have started their lectures by saying that they did not believe that religion could be so studied. William James, on the contrary, believed that this was the way to increase understanding of religion, and he enthusiastically fulfilled Lord Gifford's intention. It was as an object of scientific study that he wanted to treat religion, and the invitation to give these lectures provided him with an opportunity of doing so.

James's Gifford lectures were published in 1903 under the title: *The varieties of religious experience.*[1] This book made an immediate and lasting impression; it is one of the few psychological books of that period which is still read. A few years ago it was republished as a paper-back in the Fontana Library. Its continued popularity is, no doubt, partly due to the brilliance of William James as a writer: he was one of the last of the American psychologists to write in lively and vivid prose and it has been said of him that he wrote text-books as if they were novels. A more important factor however was, I think, a general appreciation of the importance of his method of approach which has become the standard attitude of psychological students of religion. This was guided by the idea that the essential function of the psychologist was to study and observe the phenomena of religion without concerning himself with making judgments as to the truth of its propositions or trying to appraise its values. The statement of this principle raises the question of whether one can or should study religion in this way. There is no doubt that one can adopt the aim of dispassionate study, but it is doubtful whether over the whole field of religion any writer has completely achieved it. Certainly William James did not; there is probably more appraisal in his book than its author intended. A critic might say that his chapter on saintliness is a portrayal of how mediaeval sanctity looks to a modern American.

To be fair to James, however, he must add, 'to a modern American trying hard to be just and to divest himself of his prejudices'. This is, moreover, a field in which many writers had not tried either to be just or to divest themselves of their prejudices.

The question remains, whether the aim is a worth-while one. It is undoubtedly true that dispassionate study is not all that one has to do about religion; there are also important decisions to be made as to one's own commitment. Preliminary dispassionate study may, however, contribute to make such decisions more reasonable. In addition, dispassionate study of religion has its own value in promoting the understanding of the religion of others. If it makes no direct contribution to religious enthusiasm, it does contribute to religious toleration. Both may be regarded as important. The past history of religion suggests that effort has been mostly directed towards increasing enthusiasm; psychological study should do something towards correcting the balance by increasing tolerance and mutual understanding. Religious tolerance has increased considerably since the beginning of the present century; religious differences are no longer seen as grounds for condemnation but rather as invitations to make an effort to understand. We still have a long way to go, and it remains true that mutual understanding of religious differences requires not merely good-will but also sound knowledge. Nonetheless, the work started by James may have been one of the factors in increasing religious understanding. Perhaps the day will come when the application of psychological methods of study to political differences will help the achievement of tolerance and mutual understanding even in this field.

In the thirty years following the publication of *The varieties of religious experience*, many other books were published along similar lines; I wrote one of them myself, the first edition of the present work, published in 1923.[2] It was one of a large number, each contributing something, either in point of view or in the material incorporated. What was novel in my own book was an attempt to use the conceptual system of psychoanalysis, then becoming known for the first time in Great Britain, to the elucidation of religious problems. All of these books may have contributed something towards the goal of using psychology as a means of understanding religion but as the methods employed by James could not go on indefinitely yielding new results, the writings following this tradition tended to become repetitive. A new source of material was required.

The sources primarily used by William James and his followers were the writings and biographies of religious individuals. These were selected and interpreted by the writer, who used psychological principles for their interpretation and also used these selected facts as criteria for the development of psychological principles. The first of these aims is unexceptionable; it lays the foundation for a scientific understanding of religion. This foundation may be described as the 'natural history of religion'. James's contribution was that he started the application of psychology to the task of constructing a natural history of religion; his achievement was an important one but it was limited.

Its limitation comes out most clearly in connection with the second aim mentioned above, the utilisation of facts of religion for the development of psychological principles for understanding them. The fact that the material drawn from religious writings and biographies has been selected by the author renders it unsuitable for deciding theoretical issues. Let us suppose, for example, that a writer on the psychology of religion puts forward the idea that one of the sources of religious devotion is deprivation of maternal love in childhood. One could, no doubt, find in religious literature extracts to support this contention and extracts to refute it. The author may select his extracts to support whichever opinion on the subject seems to him to be a true one. To reach a valid conclusion, some more systematic way of gathering the evidence is required. It must involve counting the number of devout persons in a sample of people who have been deprived of maternal love in childhood, and comparing it with the number of devout persons in an otherwise similar sample who have not been so deprived. If a statistical comparison of the two groups showed a significant difference between the proportions of devout persons in each, this would agree with the expectations roused by the hypothesis that early deprivation of love was one of the factors producing religious devotion. It would not be proof that this hypothesis was a true one, since there might be some other explanation of the observed relationship, for example that there was some difference in temperament between the members of the two groups which caused them to be unloved in their childhood and devout in their later years. If, on the other hand, no significant difference between the two groups were found, this would be much more definite evidence against the truth of the original hypothesis. It would not prove that deprivation of love had nothing to do with the development of religious devotion but it would show that such deprivation did not affect religious development to an appreciable extent which, in practice, is all that we need to know.

This is an imaginary example of the kind of quantitative enquiry that might be made in order to settle a disputed question in the psychology of religion. As in other branches of psychology, the psychological study of religion has become increasingly concerned in such quantitative or quasi-experimental researches since James's day. In fact, such enquiry began as early as the descriptive approach to the psychology of religion carried out by James and those who followed in his tradition. Before the close of the nineteenth century, Starbuck was making a quantitative study of religious conversion, which he published a few years later under the title *The psychology of religion*.[3]

Although this, at the time, attracted much less attention than the work of James, it was the earliest of a number of quantitative researches in the psychology of religion which would now generally be regarded by strict experimentalists as more soundly based than the brilliant speculations of William James.

Other semi-experimental though non-quantitative researches also date from before the beginning of the present century. These include the observations made by Colonel Blood and others of the emotional experiences resulting from the inhalation of nitrous oxide. Some account of these will be found in James's *Varieties*. They now have an impressive number of descendants in the studies of religious or quasi-religious experiences resulting from the use of psychedelic drugs.[4]

Many years passed after Starbuck's pioneering investigation of conversion before psychologists became generally interested in the application of the methods of experiment and exact quantitative enquiry to the problems of the psychology of religion. One of the early followers of this path was Professor Leuba of Bryn Mawr College. In 1921 he published the results of an enquiry into the percentages of those holding academic posts in various subjects who believed in God and in the immortality of the human soul.[5] He found, for example, that both beliefs were held more commonly by physicists than by psychologists. His results showed:

|  | *Believing in God* | *Believing in immortality* |
|---|---|---|
| Physicists | 44 per cent | 51 per cent |
| Psychologists | 24 | 20 |

This tells us something about the distribution of religious beliefs in the social setting and at the time of Leuba's investigation. Other investigations would be necessary in order to find out how general is the finding that physicists are more likely to have positive religious beliefs than psychologists. Unless, however, one is prepared to accept the unwarranted supposition that psychologists know more about such matters and are, therefore, more likely to be right, it seems to be of limited importance.

It is indeed one of the charges that the experimental psychologist must consider, that his contributions to the study of religion are relatively trivial. If, for example, we turn from the reading of William James's chapter on 'saintliness' to Leuba's measurements of the distribution of religious belief amongst different kinds of scientist, we seem to be turning from a treatment of a fundamental religious question to one of such peripheral interest that few people would suppose it to be of any importance.

The first part of the experimental psychologist's defence against this charge is that his purpose is to contribute assured knowledge obtained by scientific procedures and that the topics which can be illuminated in this way are often not the ones regarded as important by the theologian or by the devout person. It is plainly easier to devise methods of studying what scientists think about God and immortality than to make a scientific study of saintliness. The justification for such a study as Leuba's is that it is a single brick in the building of a psychological understanding of religion. A brick is trivial compared with the architectural plans for a building. It owes its significance to its relation with other bricks. The justification for any empirical research in the psychology of religion may be its contribution (not necessarily large) to the whole psychological understanding of religion. If it plays no part in contributing to this understanding, it is truly insignificant. Although there are no doubt such wholly insignificant researches in the psychology of religion, it must not be too readily assumed that an investigation is insignificant because its contribution to total understanding is not immediately obvious.

Some experimental enquiries do not need the justification that their significance arises from the contribution they make to a general structure for the understanding of religion. In some cases, the practical significance of an empirical enquiry is immediately obvious. Examples are to be found in Godin's researches on magical thinking in childhood,[6] and in Goldman's researches into conceptual development in children's religious thinking.[7] Both of these investigations have obvious practical implications for religious education. Other significant empirical researches on the psychology of religion may have no immediate practical implications but make a real contribution to the psychological understanding of religion. This contribution to understanding is their justification; it is not reasonable to condemn them as trivial because they may have no immediate practical importance.

Some contemporary psychologists would consider that these quantitative and experimental investigations are the only significant contributions to the psychology of religion, and that such wide surveys as that of William James, based on selected examples from religious literature or from observation of life, are of merely historical interest. I do not agree with this judgment. Both kinds of material have a part to play in the psychological understanding of religion. Mere accumulation of quantitative answers to specific questions in religious psychology may lead to very imperfect understanding of its problems unless accompanied by an adequate psychological picture of the whole field of religion, including regions where specific quantitative enquiries have not yet been made. At the same time this wider picture provided by religious literature and casual observation needs checking at particular points where a specific question can be asked. Casual observation, for example, may convince us that women show a higher level of religious conformity than men, but empirical research is necessary to find out how much higher this level is, whether it is found in all religious bodies, and whether it is correlated with some more general personality difference between the sexes.

During the last thirty or forty years, the number of such enquiries into particular problems in religious psychology has been enormous. No book could deal with all of them; a long book would be needed even to give a fair representation of the most important of them. I shall not attempt to do this here but shall give a small sample of researches which happen to deal with points I am particularly interested in. Much will be left out, but the purpose of the present book – to give a general introduction to the psychology of religion – can only be fulfilled by presenting a small sample of this large field of research.

The shift of interest from the selection of extracts from religious literature towards quantitative enquiries is not, however, the only change in method of the psychological study of religion which has taken place since James's time. There is also a shift from the study of conscious experience to the study of behaviour. No psychologist would be likely now to write a book with James's title *The varieties of religious experience*; a more likely choice would be *The varieties of religious behaviour*. The difference is perhaps less radical than it appears at first sight. What James's book was, in fact, principally concerned with was religious behaviour; with prayer behaviour, with the social behaviour of religious people, and with various aspects of their verbal behaviour. There has, however, also been a real change in emphasis; some of the topics with which James was concerned would no longer seem proper subjects for psychological enquiry to a modern behaviouristically-oriented psychologist. Such a psychologist might, for example, be impatient of James's discussion of the nature of the mystical experience, and of some of his other topics which cannot be entirely reduced to problems of behaviour.

I am not myself a behaviourist but I am sufficiently affected by the change in outlook in psychology to find some of the statements in the first edition of this book excessively subjective. I should not now, for example, entitle a chapter 'Conscious processes' as I did then. In fact, the chapter so named was not well described since it was mostly about the linguistic problems of emotional processes and dispositions, and it would not have been out of place in a rigorously behaviouristic text. Also I would not now say: 'The main business of the psychology of religion is to study the religious consciousness ... we must investigate religious behaviour as well.' I should now be inclined to invert this and say: 'The main business of the psychology of religion is to study religious behaviour.' I would, however, part company from the strict behaviourists by continuing: 'we must study the religious consciousness as well'.

Behaviourism has been useful to psychology by directing attention from mere speculation towards the solution of soluble problems, yet it has led to some loss by narrowing too much the psychologist's field of interest. The problems of consciousness neglected in the behaviourist approach remain real problems which might not be studied at all if the psychologist turned his back on them.

There has been an encouraging return to interest in these problems in recent years amongst psychologists. The changed states of consciousness produced by drugs and by meditational practices have increasingly become topics of interest to psychologists, and James's interest in them would no longer seem eccentric as it did to the behaviourists.[4] This renewed concern with problems of consciousness opens the way to a wider use of psychology in the task of understanding the problems of religion.

William James's idea that the study of religion should become a branch of natural science comes nearer to realisation as it ceases to be only an idea of solitary scholars and becomes the aim of research foundations organised for that end. An important step in this direction was taken in 1969 when Sir Alister Hardy founded in Oxford the Religious Experience Research Unit. This is too recent to have produced any reportable results, but its foundation seems to be a step in the direction of realisation of the ideals of Lord Gifford and of William James.

REFERENCES

1. W. James, *The varieties of religious experience*, London, 1902.
2. R. H. Thouless, *An introduction to the psychology of religion*, 1st ed., Cambridge, 1923.
3. E. D. Starbuck, *The psychology of religion*, New York, 1899.
4. C. Tart, (Ed.), *Altered states of consciousness*, New York and London, 1969.
5. J. H. Leuba, *The belief in God and immortality*, Boston (Mass.), 1921.
6. A. Godin and Soeur Marthe, 'Magical mentality and sacramental life in children of 8 to 14 years', *Lumen Vitae*, xv, Brussels, 1960, pp. 277–96.
7. R. Goldman, *Religious thinking from childhood to adolescence*, London, 1964.

# 2. Psychology and religion

At some stage in studying the psychology of religion, one is bound to ask what are to be understood by the words 'psychology' and 'religion'. Both words are used with some variety of meaning; this does not mean that there is an insuperable barrier to exact thinking about them; it does, however, make it necessary that a particular writer should make clear how he is going to use them.

The word 'psychology' is now generally used for the science of human behaviour and experience. This science has developed a great deal since the beginning of the present century both in its methods of enquiry and in its ways of talking about the results of its enquiries, that is, in its 'conceptual system'. Psychological investigation may be regarded as a system of techniques of enquiry directed towards the understanding of what men do, think and feel. These techniques include the experimental methods of the psychological laboratory, the use of statistical methods (such as 'factor analysis'), the use of psychological tests, enquiries by questionnaires addressed to groups of people, case history studies of particular individuals, and so on. Sometimes the data for the psychologist's enquiries will be found in printed form (as in religious autobiographies), sometimes he will collect it for himself.

Will part of the data of the psychological student of religion come from his own self observation? To many modern psychologists, an affirmative answer to this question would seem old-fashioned and to belong to the days of 'introspectionism'. Certainly it must be agreed that the psychologist's own introspections are likely to be as misleading to the psychologist studying religion as in any other field if he treats them as primary material for drawing conclusions. At the same time, it is impossible that his investigations should not be guided to a considerable extent by what he himself has experienced of a religion, either in the practising of it or in the rejection of it. It may indeed be considered that some measure of involvement in religion, whether in acceptance or rejection, is a necessary condition for research into the psychology of religion. It may even be argued that deliberate increase of the range of involvement, for instance, by engaging in the practices of other forms of religion than one's own, may increase the fruitfulness of such research.

Whatever methods of enquiry he may adopt, the psychologist's investigation of religion will be directed by one or more systems of psychological theory. A particular psychological investigator may use a theoretical form of behaviourism in which he regards the acquisition of human behaviour as a mechanical process determined by the principle that rewarded behaviour tends to be repeated. Another psychologist may adopt a voluntaristic theory which assumes that in human choice there is an element that is non-mechanical. Another may base his theory on the ideas of Freud, the inventor of psychoanalysis, who regarded behaviour as basically determined by the tendency to maximise pleasure and as influenced not only by conscious choice but also by impulses from the unconscious. It would be simpler for the psychological student if there were only one agreed body of psychological theory, but this would not necessarily provide the best instrument for the understanding of human behaviour and thought. We need not regard these theories as alternative dogmatic systems of which one may be right and the others must be wrong. Rather they can be regarded as different systems serving the end of describing and explaining different aspects of human behaviour. We have no reason for supposing that psychology will ever develop one all-inclusive theoretical system within which all the facts will be explained. Heisenberg has put forward the view that at least four theoretical systems are necessary for understanding the facts of the physical world.[1] These are systems of theoretical explanation that cannot be deduced from each other although they do not contradict each other. If four systems of theory are necessary for understanding the facts of the physical world, it seems reasonable to suppose that the much more complex facts of psychology are unlikely to become explicable in terms of a single theoretical system.

So, in applying psychology to the study of religion, we are under no obligation to embrace one of its systems of theory and to use only that. We shall probably stand a better chance of achieving psychological understanding of religious behaviour if we are willing to use a variety of the alternative language systems that are available in psychological theory. We need not consider this only a temporary expedient forced on us by the undeveloped nature of psychological science; it may be a permanent necessity resulting from the complexity of the subject matter of psychology.

The meaning of the word 'religion' arouses considerable controversy, often greater than the importance of the question warrants. We are concerned only with the way in which a word is to be used; no question of fact or value hangs on it. Certain ways of defining 'religion' are obviously inconvenient since they either leave unclear the distinction between religious and non-religious activities or they draw a line where we should not do so in ordinary speech. If, for example, we follow Hegel in defining religion as the knowledge possessed by the finite mind of its nature as absolute mind, we are making the meaning of 'religion' much narrower than it is in everyday speech, for this definition would imply that a man can only be religious if he is a philosopher. Nor can we make much use of the definition given by F. W. H. Myers, that religion is the 'sane and normal response of the human spirit to all that we know of cosmic law'.[2] This is too indefinite in its indications to serve the purpose of identifying religion; how are we to tell which of the responses men make to what they know of cosmic law is the 'sane and normal' one? It also misuses the process of definition, not identifying religion but praising it: a definition should indicate the way a word is used, not evaluate what it stands for. If this definition points to the best kind of religion, it is still necessary to have the word 'religion' as a name for the worse kinds of religion, those, for example, that may be insane and abnormal responses to what men know of cosmic law. We shall need to use the word 'religion' in an emotionally neutral sense in order to allow us to say that there may be good and bad sorts of religion.

When J. H. Leuba wrote a book on the psychology of religion, he included an appendix which listed forty-eight different definitions of religion given by various writers.[3] This does not, however, imply that the meaning of 'religion' is so obscure that we cannot hope to think clearly about it. The variety of definitions seems to have its source partly in disagreement between different writers as to how they want to use the word, partly in disagreement as to how they want to embody in a definition such meaning as is agreed. Every writer must decide which of the possible meanings of the word 'religion' he is going to adopt, and try to express that chosen meaning as clearly as he can in a definition.

The rule for making a definition laid down long ago by Aristotle is that it should indicate the class to which the object defined belongs together with the special characteristic which distinguishes it from other members of the same class, as when we define a mammal as an animal that suckles its young. Although we know very well how to use some words we may not find it easy to indicate that use by a neat formal definition. Wittgenstein has pointed out that 'game' is such a word,[4] 'religion' is, no doubt, another.

Formal definition is, however, only one of the devices for indicating the way we intend to use a word. If the word is (like 'religion') the name of a class, we can indicate its meaning by giving a representative sample of members of that class. We can say for example, that 'religion' is the name of a class including Christianity, Islam, Theosophy, Judaism, Buddhism and so on.

This is, at any rate, a first approach to making clear the use of the word. It leaves some uncertainty, since we do not know exactly what other members are included in the words 'and so on'. Certainly Hinduism, but what about Communism? This question is not very important; it is a matter on which one may make a decision either way. The ordinary use of the word will not generally be affected by our choice; it is important only that we should be consistent in the use we have chosen. 'Religion' is a word particularly liable to be used with shifting meanings which produce muddled thinking.

To avoid the possibility of such muddle may be a sound reason for attempting the task of defining 'religion' by the formal Aristotelian method. Here too a choice must be made; one person's definition may differ from another's because they adopt different uses of the word. Neither may be wrong in the sense that he defines a use outside the range of variation of meaning found in everyday language. Both have the duty to make their own use of the term clear so that any difference between them that results from a difference in the way they are using a word shall not be mistaken for a difference as to fact.

Some of the diversity in the definitions of 'religion' noted by Leuba seems to be due less to difference of opinion as to how the word should be used than to a lack of clarity as to how a definition should be constructed. Some of the definitions refer to religion as a mode of behaviour, some as a system of belief, and some as a particular emotion. It seems more consistent with the way the word is commonly used to say that it covers all of these things, that the general class to which religion belongs is one that includes a mode of behaviour, a system of beliefs, and a system of feelings. So, in the first edition of the present book, I gave as my definition: 'Religion is a felt practical relationship with what is believed in as a superhuman being or beings.'

I am not inclined to defend this definition now. Certainly it had the merit of emphasising the important point that a religion is a system which includes a special way of behaving and of feeling, and a special system of beliefs, although it did so in a rather clumsy way. The point could have been made more neatly by the use of the word 'attitude', which is a generally accepted term for a disposition which includes characteristic ways of behaving, feeling, and believing. If this term is used, religion can be defined as a particular kind of attitude towards the world as a whole.

The question that remains is what is the special characteristic of an attitude towards the world as a whole that makes us call it a religious one. In my first definition, I took this characteristic to be the fact that a religious attitude was centred round a belief in God or in gods. I do not now think that this criterion is, in any sense, wrong, but I no longer consider that it is convenient. It makes discrimination difficult where personal characteristics are denied to the deity, as in the *advaita* form of the Hindu religion. Also it has the disadvantage of excluding Buddhism from the class of religions, not because superhuman beings are non-existent in the teaching of the Buddha but because he taught that they too were transitory and not to be worshipped or made objects of religious trust. One can, of course, accept this exclusion of Buddhism from the category of religions, and say that Buddhism is a non-religious spiritual therapeutic system. One would have to say something of that sort if one confined the use of the word 'religion' to attitudes centred round a superhuman being or beings. To say this would, however, do some violence to the generally accepted use of the word 'religion', and it would be somewhat misleading since it would direct attention away from the very important respects in which Buddhism is plainly a member of the same class as Islam, Christianity, Judaism, etc.

The main respect in which all these systems resemble one another and in which they differ from such an attitude as that of scientific naturalism is that they consider that the world of space and time in which our bodies live is not the only part of our environment to which we must be adjusted. They believe that there is also some kind of spiritual world which makes demands on our behaviour, our thinking, and our feeling. This other world is very variously conceived by the different religions and may be very differently inhabited, but some form of such a world is always a dominant element in what determines the religious attitude.

The presence of some kind of other-worldliness may be illustrated in a wide range of religious faiths. In Judaism, for example, a typical statement is that of the 33rd psalm: 'The Lord looks down from heaven, he sees all the sons of men; from where he sits enthroned he looks forth on all the inhabitants of the earth.'[5] In the teachings of Jesus Christ as recorded in the Gospels, there are numerous references to a spiritual world: 'In my Father's house are many rooms; if it were not so, would I have told you that I go to prepare a place for you?' (John 14.2). 'Do you think that I cannot appeal to my Father, and he will at once send me more than twelve legions of angels?' (Matt. 26.53). 'And if God so clothes the grass of the field, which today is alive and tomorrow is thrown into the oven, will he not much more clothe you, O men of little faith?' (Matt. 6.32). In the teaching of the Buddha too we find references to a spiritual world. He is reported to have opposed the views of those ascetics and Brahmins who held that there is no such thing as this world or a world beyond: 'Assuredly, there really is a world beyond; the belief that there is no such world, that is a false view.'[6]

If it is agreed that some form of 'other-worldliness' is an essential characteristic of all the systems of behaviour and thought that we are inclined to call 'religions', this element may be considered the most convenient distinguishing criterion to use in a definition of religion. We can then suggest the following definition: *religion is an attitude (or mode of adjustment) to the world which includes reference to a wider environment than that of the spatio–temporal physical world (i.e. to a spiritual world).*

It is obvious that this definition does not, and is not intended to, make the word 'religion' cover the whole class of attitudes towards the world that deserve esteem. Men can be virtuous and self-sacrificing without being, in the sense defined, religious. The definition has, I think, the merit of including under the name 'religion' attitudes that would in every-day speech be called 'religious' and excluding those which we should ordinarily call 'irreligious'. It does so, I think, better than the definition I offered in the first edition of this book. It includes, for example, Buddhism and Spiritualism but it excludes Communism and Humanism. I do not, of course, maintain that this is the one right definition; only that it describes the use I am making of the word 'religion' in the present book.

It is also to be noted in its favour that this appears to be the meaning attached to the word 'religion' by those Christian writers who follow Bonhoeffer in thinking of the future of their faith as 'Christianity without religion'.[7] The element which is in their opinion to be discarded from Christianity is its other-worldliness, the 'conception of a supernatural order which invades and "perforates" this one'.[8] The psychologist has no special right to judge whether this element ought or ought not to be discarded; I myself think not. Our concern here is only to note that, in referring to its elimination as 'the elimination of the religious element' in Christianity, these writers appear to be using the word 'religion' in the way in which it has been here defined. It would seem to follow that if any body of Christians did evolve so far in this direction that their Christianity was wholly non-religious, their ways of behaving, thinking, and feeling, although still of interest to the psychologist, would cease to be part of the subject matter of a book on the psychology of religion.

If we give up the fact that it is centred round a God or gods as the defining criterion of religion, it remains true that those religions which are so centred form an important sub-class of the religions. We need a term to distinguish these, and for this purpose we can use the commonly accepted term 'theistic religions'. The use of this term does not imply that the theistic and non-theistic religions are sharply separated from one another or that a single religion may not have theistic and non-theistic strands. The theistic religions may be further subdivided into those that are mono-theistic, such as Judaism and Islam, and those that are poly-theistic as are many primitive religions. Again there is no sharp dividing line between the classes. The common people of a religious tradition may be poly-theistic while its sages worship only one God. The dividing line may be further confused by the acceptance of the idea that the many gods are all aspects of the one god. The other world may be populated with powerful beings (such as the angels of the Jewish–Christian tradition) who are not regarded as gods. This raises the difficult question of what level of knowledge, power and goodness a superhuman being must be supposed to have to be regarded as a god, or alternatively what kind of behaviour men must adopt towards him to make us say that he is treated as a god. In many respects the dividing line between monotheistic and polytheistic religions is not sharp, yet the psychological difference between them is important. A classification may be useful even if it lacks sharp boundaries.

The psychology of religion as a branch of enquiry should be distinguished from the comparative study of religions. Both have the aim of increasing the understanding of religion by applying to it the methods of a non-religious, non-theological, type of investigation. The comparative study of religions, however, tends to be concerned with primitive and exotic religions rather than with the religion of our own culture. Its aim is to advance understanding by comparing one religion with another, whereas the psychological study of religions is concerned rather to understand religious behaviour by applying to it the psychological principles derived from the study of non-religious behaviour. The present work will therefore be concerned with the more developed religions rather than with the primitive ones, and will deal in particular with the various forms of Christianity we are likely to meet in our own culture and by which we are likely to be influenced in various ways whether we accept or reject them. Sometimes, a psychological point will be illuminated by a citation from the literature of some religion other than Christianity, or a psychological question in connection with Christianity may suggest a comparison with some other religion. In such cases, a reference will be made to that other religion, but the aim will be primarily to increase understanding of the religious problems of our own culture and not to make a contribution to comparative religion.

## REFERENCES

1. W. Heisenberg, *Physics and philosophy*, New York, 1958.
2. F. W. H. Myers, *Human personality and its survival of bodily death*, vol. 2, London, 1903.
3. J. H. Leuba, *A psychological study of religion*, New York, 1912.
4. L. Wittgenstein, *Philosophical investigations*, Oxford, 1953.
5. *The Holy Bible*, Revised Standard Version, 1952.
6. *Apannaka Sutta* (English translation by Narada Thera and Mahinda Thera), Kandy, 1966.
7. D. Bonhoeffer, *Letters and papers from prison*, London, 1953.
8. J. A. T. Robinson, *Honest to God*, London, 1963.

# 3. The psychological roots of religion

At the beginning of a psychological study of religion, one may be tempted to follow the false track that starts with the question: 'What is the psychological root of religion?' One suggested answer may be that man's religion is rooted in his sexuality or his helplessness in a hostile environment, and that his religious beliefs and behaviour are to be understood as transformed expressions of these primitive needs. Other writers may suggest different roots of religion such as man's occasional ecstatic awareness of his oneness with nature, or his processes of verbal thinking about the problems of the world around him or his own moral conflicts. Any of these may be put forward as the single source and origin of the religions of men. This way of thinking is perhaps less common now than it was forty years ago; it remains, I think, a pitfall on the road to the psychological understanding of religion. Any or all of these factors may play a part in the causation of religion; the pitfall lies in the tendency to say that one of them is the sole factor.

The idea of a single psychological root of religious belief and behaviour is now perhaps more often assumed than explicitly stated. Many religious philosophers write as if they held the old view put forward by St Anselm that the existence of God could be proved by a process of reasoning and that the acceptance of such reasoning could be a sufficient psychological ground for religious belief. Some writers maintain that one can have an intuitive certainty of the reality of the objects of religion which cannot be rationally proved but which they cannot doubt. Some rest their religious faith on the authority of the Church or of the Bible. Some feel the importance of the demands of morality, and find the sanction for them in the conception of a supreme lawgiver. Some point to the beauty of nature and find in this the signature of a loving creator. All of these may be factors in the development of the religious attitude; none can plausibly be regarded as its sole origin. Religion is a complex structure which may have many roots. If, instead of asking the question in its singular form: 'What is the psychological root of religion?', we put it more tentatively into a plural form and asked: 'What might be the psychological roots of religion?', we should have a more promising starting point for a psychological enquiry into religion.

If we try to classify the factors which have been or may be claimed to produce the religious attitude, they seem to fall into four main groups: social influences, experiences, needs, and processes of thought. The first may be called the *social* factor; it includes all the social influences in the development of the religious attitude: parental teaching, social traditions, and the pressures of the social environment towards conformity with the opinions and attitudes approved by that environment. The psychological concept which bears most closely on such influences is that of *suggestion*. Many of those who have discussed the social factor in religious development have been inclined to treat it as the sole root of the religious attitude of most people, maintaining that, with the exception of a few creative individuals, the religious opinions of men are at second-hand. No doubt they very largely are; the social factor is an influential one in social development. But there seems no reason for supposing that the influence of other factors is confined to few individuals. It seems likely that more ordinary people do not merely receive a religious tradition passively but react with what is socially received in such a way that it is made to fit in with their own experiences and their own needs.

In addition therefore, we are concerned with the kinds of experience and need that can contribute to the religious attitude. It has commonly been thought that the felt presence of beauty, harmony and beneficence in the external world plays a part in the production of the religious attitude. We may consider this as a possible psychological factor in the development of the religious attitude without committing ourselves to any judgment as to whether it is a rational ground for defending religious belief. In contrast to the experiences of beauty, harmony and beneficence, there are also experiences of ugliness, disorder and malevolence. This contrast renders possible the development of a dualist element in the religious attitude, as, for example, when a good superhuman being is considered to be on one side and an evil person or force on the other.

Another contrast between a pair of opposites that may play a part in the development of the religious attitude is the experience of moral conflict, i.e. of the conflict between the behaviour impulses which the individual regards as leading him in a right direction and those which seem to him to be wrong. This conflict too can lead to dualism in the religious attitude, since the right impulses can be regarded as those in accordance with the will of God while the wrong impulses belong to forces in the spiritual world which are opposed to God.

In addition to experiences of the natural or of the moral order, there is also a range of inner emotional experiences which seem more directly connected with God or with some other object of the religious attitude. These inner experiences are sometimes called simply 'religious experiences' although it seems preferable to use this term in a somewhat wider sense. These inner experiences may be studied in their most dramatic form in the literature of religious mysticism. There is, however, no good reason for regarding them as belonging only to the mystical tradition; they may be a factor in the experience of all religious individuals. Those to whom social factors have given a theistic kind of religion are inclined to interpret such feelings as experiences of God. This interpretation, however, does not seem to belong to them intrinsically; the non-theist may report what seem to be similar experiences which he interprets in a non-theistic (impersonal) way. This, however, is quite consistent with the possibility that the personal, theistic, interpretation of such quasi-mystical experiences is the most natural one in the sense that they seem like experiences of communication with a person.

These three kinds of experience which we shall consider in later chapters as possible factors in the formation of a religious attitude may conveniently be called the *natural,* the *moral*, and the *affective* factors in religion.

Another factor which various writers have treated as the source of religious belief is the existence of needs not fully satisfied elsewhere which creates a felt need for religious satisfactions. These may be grouped under four headings: the need for security, the need for love, the need for self-esteem, and the need created by the inevitability of death. Most of these needs have, from time to time, been postulated as the sole source of religious belief. Each may, I think, be reasonably considered as a possible factor in the development of the religious attitude.

The last factor to be considered is the part played in the development of the religious attitude by verbal reasoning. There is a popular opinion, reflected in many polemical writings on religion, that this factor plays a much larger part in the formation of religious opinion than would be considered likely by any psychologist. Such writings seem often to assume that the arguments that men bring forward in favour of their religious beliefs are their reasons for holding them and that the arguments other men direct against religious beliefs are their reasons for rejecting them. No doubt the fact that one can bring forward a satisfying argument in favour of an opinion is part of the situation which enables one to hold that opinion, but no psychologist would now suppose that it was sufficient in itself to account for the opinion. He would expect that a large part in the formation of opinions would be played by such irrational factors as needs and feelings, and that these would often be the primary factors in determining beliefs, while intellectual processes played only a secondary part by providing an apparently rational justification for opinions held mainly on other grounds.

The term 'rationalisation' has been very commonly adopted to describe the process of developing intellectual justification for beliefs really held on irrational grounds. There is no doubt that such a process exists and that a person may be unaware of the irrational determinant of his belief and suppose that the intellectual grounds he gives are his real reasons for holding it. He may, for example, uphold the idea of human immortality because he is afraid of extinction. Acceptance of this principle does not, of course, enable us to determine whether the belief in question is correct or not; his neighbour may argue equally strongly against survival because he is afraid of continued existence. The acceptance of rationalisation as a genuine psychological process does, however, give a reason for careful scrutiny of arguments used in connection with beliefs about matters on which men have strong feelings.

If it appeared that the only function of the intellect in the formation of religious beliefs was rationalisation, there would be little reason for postulating an *intellectual factor* as one of the elements which may contribute to the religious attitude. There seem, however, to be insufficient grounds for holding such an extreme view of the effect of thought processes on belief. Man is a thinking animal, and one of the results of his thinking is that it helps him to determine which beliefs he accepts and which ones he rejects, even though other factors also help to determine this. Some people develop a system of religious beliefs partly as a result of intellectual processes, while others are led to reject the religious attitude because it seems to them that there are intel- lectual grounds for rejecting beliefs they regard as essential to it. Many Victorian novels dealt with the intellectual struggles of devout men who felt themselves forced to give up their Christian faith because they could not believe in the historical truth of the story of creation in the Book of Genesis, or in the bodily resurrection of Jesus Christ.[1] Although less popular as a subject for fiction, there are also records of similar conflicts in religious unbelievers who have found what seem to them to be rational grounds for rejecting their previous non-religious attitude and accepting some system of religious belief.[2] In both of these cases it is likely that the struggles were initiated partly by other factors, but reasoning processes played their own important part in the conflict and its ultimate resolution. There seem to be sufficient indications that the rational factor should be considered as one of the many factors operative in the forming (or in the destruc- tion) of a religious attitude, although it is easy to over-estimate the part it plays.

It has been suggested above that we may distinguish a number of possible factors in the development of a religious attitude. These will be discussed in more detail in later chapters. They may be sum- marised as follows:

1. The influence of teaching and various social pressures (the *social* factor).

2. Various kinds of experience contributing to the religious attitude, especially those of:

(a) beauty, harmony, and beneficence in the outside world (the *natural* factor);

(b) the experience of moral conflict (the *moral* factor);

(c) religious emotional experience (the *affective* factor).

3. The factors arising from wholly or partially unsatisfied needs, in particular the needs for:

(a) *security*;

(b) *love*;

(c) *self-esteem*;

(d) *reassurance about death.*

4. Verbal processes of thought (the *intellectual* factor).

Any such listing of the factors which may play a part in the production of the religious attitude must be regarded as tentative. Its primary purpose is to act as a guide to later investigation. The method of investigation particularly appropriate to this problem is that of factor analysis. When such investigation is carried out, it may confirm the reality of some of the suggested factors but not all of them; it is almost certain also to indicate other factors not mentioned in the above list. This is not put forward as a solution of the problem of the analysis of the origins of the religious attitude, but simply as a hypothesis which will be used to guide the present study.

REFERENCES

1. Mary A. Ward, *Robert Elsmere*, London, 1888.
2. C. E. M. Joad, *The recovery of belief*, London, 1952.

# 4. The social factor in religion

The social factor in religion is made up of the various influences on religious belief and behaviour of the teaching we receive in childhood, the opinions and attitudes of those around us, and the traditions we receive from the past. We may be tempted to regard this factor as less important in our own religious development than the psychologist considers it. None of us develop our religious attitudes in isolation from our fellow men; from childhood to old age we are receiving from the behaviour of those around us and from what is said by them influences that affect our religious attitudes. It is not only our beliefs that are influenced by social factors. Our patterns of emotional expression too may be moulded to a considerable extent by our social environment. The members of a religious group for which adolescent conversion is the accepted pattern of religious behaviour, all tend during adolescence to go through a series of emotional experiences which they describe in similar terms. These experiences may be absent from another community with different traditions of how adolescent conversion should take place. The pattern appears to be a product of the social conventions of the community in which they are found.

Social factors are also apparent in the formation of religious belief, but it is not principally through reasoned demonstration that the beliefs of an individual are influenced by other people. Reasoning no doubt plays a part in the mutual interaction of people's belief systems, but its role is much smaller than that of other, non-rational, psychological processes. No one supposes that the way to teach a young child about God is to produce a rational argument for the existence of God. Teaching comes first; the time for rational arguments comes later. In later life too, the affirmation of religious propositions by a respected individual (particularly if his affirmation is repeated and confident) may have a greater influence on the religious attitudes of his hearers than any chain of reasoning. The term commonly used by psychologists for this method, by which beliefs and attitudes are transmitted otherwise than by reasoned demonstration, is *suggestion*. In order that we may understand the social factor in religion, we must examine the psychology of suggestion.

The term was originally used by psychologists for a process

observed in experiments in hypnotism. A hypnotiser may, for example, show a hypnotised subject a plain pack of cards and tell him that there is a photograph of his brother on one of them. If he succeeds in getting the subject to report that he sees such a picture and to behave as if this were the case, the subject is said to have accepted the suggestion of the hypnotiser. The suggestion may also be the performance of some action, the development of or removal of some bodily disability, or the acceptance or rejection of some belief. In all such cases of successful suggestion, the idea suggested by the hypnotiser has become real to the subject as a perception, as an action, or as a belief.

There have been found to be differences in the ease with which individuals could be made to accept and realise such suggestions, and also in the ease with which they could be hypnotised. These are called differences in their *suggestibility*, the highly suggestible individual being the one who is easily hypnotised and easily led to accept and realise suggested ideas. Differences in suggestibility seem to be largely temperamental differences and may be inborn or acquired in the subject's early psychological history. They are also partly dependent on the extent to which the subject has previously been hypnotised or otherwise subjected to the process of suggestion. The successful induction of suggestion makes the subject more suggestible, and in particular more receptive to suggestions later received from the same operator. This fact should not be forgotten in evaluating the process of suggestion as a means of communicating religious ideas.

In the ordinary life situation in which religious communication occurs we do not, of course, meet with such striking phenomena as those of the hypnotist's consulting room. A normal person, not under hypnotic influence, cannot, for example, be made to see a picture on a plain card however confidently he is told that one is there. At the same time, one does find in every-day life mental processes of acceptance of communicated ideas which seem to differ from hypnotic processes only in degree. In salesmanship and in propaganda, ideas (of the merits of soap flakes or of the evils of communism) are presented in such a way that they germinate in the minds of their hearers and finally produce an action or a belief. It is now usual to extend the meaning of the word 'suggestion' to include all such cases in which a statement is made in such a manner as to cause it to be accepted by a hearer without rational ground for believing in its truth or in the credibility of the person making it. We may then define 'suggestion' as *a process of communication resulting in the acceptance and realisation of a communicated idea in the absence of adequate rational grounds for its acceptance.*

The actual techniques of the salesman or propagandist are much the same as those of the hypnotist – repeated affirmation in a confident manner. The effectiveness of suggestion is also increased by any factor that enhances the status and authority of the operator, which is no doubt one of the functions of such status symbols as degrees and titles of honour.

An extreme example of the successful use of suggestion as a means of religious propaganda is to be found in a little book called *Stories of grace*.[1]

After a sermon by the revivalist Mr Brownlow North, a young man said to him: 'I have heard your sermon, sir, and I have heard you preach often now, and I neither care for you nor your preaching, unless you can tell me, Why did God permit sin in the world?' 'Then I'll tell you,' the preacher at once replied.

> God permitted sin because He chose to do so ... If you continue to question and cavil at God's dealings and, vainly puffed up by your own carnal mind, strive to be wise above what is written, I will tell you something more that God will choose to do. He will some day choose to put you into hell! It is vain, sir, for a man to strive with his Maker; you cannot resist Him; and neither your opinion of His dealings nor your blasphemous expressions of them will in the least lessen the pain of your everlasting damnation.

This violent use of suggestion techniques seems to have had the intended effect, since a week later the young man expressed himself thus:

> I am happy, oh! so happy, sir; and though the devil comes sometimes to tempt me with my old thoughts and to ask me what reason I have to think God has forgiven me, I have always managed to get him away by telling him that I do not want to judge things any longer by my own reason, but by God's word.

We do not, of course, know the later history of this case or how permanent the change was. Such extreme reliance on authoritative suggestion and suppression of the exercise of intellectual processes seems likely to result in instability of the induced change. Where statistics of revivalism have been obtained, a large proportion of 'backsliding' is reported. Suggestion by oratory is a dramatically impressive force but its effects do not generally last very long.

While Mr North's use of the irrational forces of suggestion for inducing religious change and his uncompromising opposition to rational processes in connection with religion are, no doubt, extreme, the general principle of the usefulness of suggestion techniques is recognised by many other preachers who aim at dramatic conversions. The suggestive value of a confident manner could not be better expressed by a sceptical psychologist than it was by the revivalist Dr Torrey.[2]

> Revival preaching to be effective must be positive. The doubter never has revivals ... A revival is a revolution in many important

respects; and revolutions are never brought about by timid, fearful or deprecatory addresses. They are awakened by men who are cocksure of their ground, and who speak with authority ... Revival preaching must be directed towards the heart and not the head ... Get hold of the heart and the head yields easily.

Dr Torrey's book also contains an address by Spurgeon to open-air preachers, exhorting them to be assiduous in preaching. This is an excellent example of the use of repeated affirmation:

Go on with your preaching. Cobbler, stick to your last; preacher stick to your preaching. In the great day, when the muster roll shall be read, of all those who are converted through fine music, and church decoration, and religious exhibitions and entertainments, they will amount to the tenth part of nothing; but it will always please God by the foolishness of preaching to save them that believe. Keep to your preaching; and if you do anything beside, do not let it throw your preaching into the background. In the first place preach and in the second place preach and in the third place preach.

Believe in preaching the love of Christ, believe in preaching the atoning sacrifice, believe in preaching the new birth, believe in preaching the whole counsel of God. The old hammer of the Gospel will still break the rock in pieces; the ancient fire of Pentecost will still burn among the multitude ... Go on! go on! go on! In God's name, go on! for if the preaching of the Gospel does not save men, nothing will.

If one analyses the method of oratorical presentation used here by Spurgeon, one realises that there is neither progressive development of the thought nor any argument in support of it. Basically the method is repeated affirmation; either directly or metaphorically the same suggestion has been repeated no less than twenty-one times in the course of nine sentences. When one is aware of the method being used, the reading of the passage is unlikely to move one much. It probably had much more effect on his original hearers who were not aware of the device being used, and on whom the suggestive effect was reinforced by the fervid confidence with which Spurgeon delivered it, and by his great reputation.

It is interesting to note that successful speaking of this kind depends in part on the power of the speaker to receive suggestions from his audience. Some degree of suggestibility on the part of the speaker is one of the conditions for successful oratory; the speaker is continually responding to his audience and is constantly aware of the way in which his words are being received. He varies his method of presentation in accordance with his perception of the audience's responses. If he wants to present ideas that are new to his audience or ideas to which they may be hostile, he is aware of whether these will be accepted, and may defer saying them until a late stage of his address when the audience has become habituated to receiving his suggestions. It is probable that most successful speakers know of this need to be in emotional contact with their audiences; many ineffective speakers obviously do not. An account of the methods of Evan Roberts, a Welsh revivalist of the early part of the twentieth century, says: 'He makes the audience reveal itself, and then tells the people what they know already?'[3] Even an elaborately prepared discourse is likely to be relatively ineffective if the delivery is not controlled by affective interchange between speaker and audience.

If we say that the religious orator may be using suggestion as one of his means of influencing people, we clearly do not mean that his audience are hypnotised. They may, however, be in the condition of heightened suggestibility which we may call the *hypnoidal state*. Hypnosis proper is an artificially produced condition resembling sleep; the hypnoidal state is a condition resembling the state of half-waking which commonly precedes or follows sleep. Both may be conditions of high suggestibility; both may be induced artificially by certain kinds of stimulus, bright points of light, continuous or rhythmically varying sounds, or simply by verbal suggestions. Various factors may be present in a church service which tend to have the effect, whether intended or not, of inducing the hypnoidal state: a monotonous voice in the delivery of the words of the service, the rhythmical sounds of music and singing, and bright points of candle-light. Suggestibility may also be increased by factors emphasising the prestige of the minister such as the wearing of special clothes and the occupation of an elevated position.

Other factors affecting the suggestibility of the audience may be provided by the social situation in which the suggestions are being given. The concept of suggestion is applied not only to the situation in which one person – such as a salesman or a preacher – is producing effects on the behaviour and beliefs of others, but also to that in which a group of people is producing such effects on one or more individuals. This factor of group-suggestion may in itself produce a belief or an action, as when we hold beliefs unquestioningly because they are the beliefs of the community to which we belong; it may reinforce a suggestion received from an individual, as when a public speaker produces stronger conviction in an individual hearer because other members of the audience are showing by their behaviour that they are themselves moved by the speaker or that they are in agreement with him. This group factor in suggestion in the preaching situation may be enhanced by the congregation emphasising their group unity by making ritual gestures or spontaneous ejaculations such as 'Hallelujah' or 'Praise the Lord'.

There has been a good deal of loose thinking and writing about group suggestion. It was started by the French writer LeBon, whose work on *The crowd* is a somewhat superficial collection of anecdotes about the suggestibility, lack of responsibility, and cruelty of crowds which are used to build up a case against democracy.[4] The first confusion to be resolved if we are to think clearly about this question is that between crowds and other types of human grouping. The essential feature of a crowd is that it is a social group whose members are temporarily in physical contiguity and whose group unity depends on that physical contiguity as well as on any common purpose that they may have. Other kinds of human group, such as a society, a church, or a political party do not depend on physical contiguity. To such groups, the term 'crowd' cannot properly be applied, and no property (such as irresponsibility) can be attributed to such groups merely because it is said to be found in crowds. Both kinds of group may exert pressures on the beliefs and behaviour of their members but they are pressures of different kinds although both may be included in the concept of 'group suggestion'. It is only the pressures exerted by temporary contiguous groups that can be referred to as 'crowd suggestion'.

The term 'herd suggestion' has also been used in this sense. The justification for this term lies in the idea that the forces of social suggestion depend on the fact that man is a gregarious animal and that his group behaviour is based on the system of instincts that bind a herd of animals together.[5] It does seem that man's tendency to conform to the beliefs and behaviour demands of the society to which he belongs or of the temporary group in which he finds himself is, in part, based on his gregarious system of instincts. It is also true however that his social behaviour is largely a learned system of responses, and his group behaviour largely the result of how he has learned to behave in groups. For this reason, the term 'herd suggestion' is not now much used, and it is preferable to use the term 'group suggestion' for the general tendency of an individual's behaviour and thought to be influenced by the group to which he belongs, and 'crowd suggestion' in the more restricted sense of the influence on him of the people by whom he is physically surrounded.

It is particularly in the situation of the religious revival that one is concerned with the forces of crowd suggestion. Revivals are preaching services directed towards inducing the hearers to declare their faith in the saving power of Christ or their acceptance of Jesus Christ as their personal saviour. After an address dealing with some aspect of this invitation to faith, the audience are invited to come forward to make this declaration. They may be urged to do so by the preacher repeating in confident and slightly monotonous tones some form of invitation, such as: 'Jesus calls you. Come. Come. Come now.' The audience may be asked also to bow their heads and to sing with their **eyes** closed. The closed eyes, the monotonous singing, and the repetition of the word come, tend to produce in the audience an approach to the hypnoidal state. It may be noticed in such services that there is frequently a considerable time during which the invitation is repeated but no-one responds by coming up to the front. The forces of crowd suggestion are, however, being reinforced by the singing of the congregation who may be repeating a verse of a hymn which expresses the idea of giving oneself to Christ. When a few individuals start moving forward, the force of crowd suggestion becomes fully operative and numbers go forward and make their surrender. Some, no doubt, are starting a new kind of life with a new orientation, others are only making an emotional gesture which will have no lasting effect on their lives.

One must not exaggerate the effectiveness with which the forces of suggestion can be used in the service of religion. The ordinary religious preacher addressing the same congregation Sunday after Sunday may use a confident manner and repetition without much affecting the members of his congregation. They listen to him on Sundays but their week-day behaviour shows no particular effect of his exhortations. Instead of being influenced by suggestion they are showing the effect of 'habituation'; the stimulus which initially would have produced a behaviour response has, by its habitual occurrence ceased to produce any response. The forcible methods of the revival preacher are an attempt to use the forces of suggestion in a new way which will overcome this habituation. In the end, of course, the individual may be habituated also to the situation of revival services. He may go to them frequently and enjoy them and undergo the emotional crisis which leads to the act of surrender, but only as part of his habitual religious life without any radical re-direction.

One of the revival preacher's techniques for overcoming the effects of habituation is the production of emotional stress. Fear used to be the emotion most frequently induced by oratory, especially fear induced by vivid descriptions of hell. The following is an extract from a sermon by Jonathan Edwards, who preached in America in the early part of the eighteenth century:

We can conceive but little of the matter; but to help your conception, imagine yourselves to be cast into a fiery oven, or a great furnace, where your pain would be as much greater than that occasioned by accidentally touching a coal of fire as the heat is greater. Imagine also that your body were to lie there for a quarter of an hour, full of fire and all the while full of quick sense. What horror would you feel at the entrance of such a furnace. How long would that quarter of an hour seem to you? ... And how much greater would be the effect, if you knew you must endure it for a whole year. And how vastly greater still, if you knew you must endure it for a thousand years. Oh! then how would your heart sink if you knew that you must bear it for ever and ever – that there would be no end, that for millions and millions of ages, your torments would be no nearer to an end and that you never, never would be delivered.[1]

It is reported that the terror which gripped his audiences was such that they cried aloud for mercy and grasped their benches to prevent themselves from slipping into the pit. It is unlikely that a modern audience would respond in this way and attempts to induce strong fear by descriptions of hell are no longer common in sermons, though they went on for a long time after Jonathan Edwards. J. B. Pratt quotes from a sermon by an evangelist in New York in 1907: 'I preach hell because God puts His special blessing on it, convicting sinners and sanctifying believers ... Hell has been running for six thousand years. It is filling up every day. Where is it? About eighteen miles from here. Which way is it? Straight down – not over eighteen miles, down in the bowels of the earth.'[6]

If a modern preacher used Jonathan Edwards' way of trying to arouse fear, he would probably produce disgust or amusement. Yet the element of emotional stress may not be altogether absent from a parallel appeal at the present day; if people are no longer afraid of hell, they have, not far below the surface of their consciousness, a strong anxiety about nuclear weapons. I have heard a number of addresses by Dr Billy Graham who is perhaps the most widely known evangelist of the present day. I have not heard him refer to hell; although no doubt he believes in the reality of hell fire, he does not use it as a means of producing emotional stress in his audiences. He does, however, refer to the danger of the hydrogen bomb, and such references may produce sufficient anxiety in his audiences to increase their suggestibility to his message.

The emotional stress induced by revivalist preachers in the eighteenth and nineteenth centuries may largely explain certain abnormal effects, closely resembling convulsive attacks of hysteria, often found to accompany such preaching. The forces of crowd suggestion active in such gatherings seem also to have played a part in their production since they were easily transmitted from one person to another, and whole multitudes were reported to have fallen down, to have jerked their bodies in extraordinary contortions, and to have laughed, danced, and barked.[7] Sceptics who were present at the meetings might also find themselves affected in the same way. The following is an example quoted from Davenport of a camp-meeting of nearly 20,000 people which went on for several days:

The whole body of persons who actually fell helpless to the earth during the progress of the meeting was computed ... to be three thousand persons, about one in every six ... At no time was the floor less than half covered. Some lay quiet, unable to move or speak. Some talked, but could not move. Some beat the floor with their heels. Some, shrieking in agony, bounded about like a live fish out of water. Many lay down and rolled over and over for hours at a time. Others rushed wildly over the stumps and benches, and then plunged, shouting, 'Lost! Lost!' into the forest. (Others jerked their bodies or barked like dogs). ... Many of these camp-meeting folk lay insensible, sometimes for hours, but when they recovered from the swoon it was to relate, in what were called strains of heaven, experiences of interviews with departed friends and visions of glory.[7]

If these phenomena were peculiar to the camp-meetings of Kentucky, they might be regarded as too unusual for serious notice. Similar phenomena do, however, tend to recur in religious revivals even when they are not welcomed by those conducting the revivals. Emotional stress has been produced in revival preaching in England and sometimes it has had somewhat similar effects. John Wesley did not employ the fear of hell for the production of emotional stress as freely as did Jonathan Edwards and the camp preachers of Kentucky, but there are records of sermons by him with a great deal of hell fire in them. Two of his disciples succeeded, near Cambridge, in producing by their preaching such effects of terror that the account of it given in Wesley's diary seems more like the record of an outbreak of mental disorder than of a state induced for religious ends.[8] Such phenomena as jerks and dancing seem rather to be products of heightened suggestibility than of induced fear since they may be found in cases where the fear motive is not used, as in the Welsh revivals conducted by Evan Roberts.[3] While some revival preachers have regarded such symptoms as evidence of the working of grace, others (as, for example, Spurgeon) have considered that they are the work of the devil.

The fact that such phenomena may be accepted as evidence of the working of divine grace leads to the possibility that they may come to be regarded as normal and desirable accompaniments of religious activity. There are some religious bodies (especially in America) where the usual Sunday services are accompanied by such phenomena as automatisms of speech and behaviour: ejaculations, jerking, dancing, etc. which are regarded as evidence of the coming of the Holy Spirit to the congregation.

Religious services of this type will be further discussed in Chapter 7. Such services must not be confused with revival services; their aim is different. They are not intended to produce conversion which is an event that is supposed to happen only once to the same individual. In these cases, the induced emotional experience happens Sunday after Sunday to the same individual; it is a recurrent experience, not (like conversion) a culminating one.

The Kentucky revivals followed a typical pattern which is recognisable to some degree in the majority of religious services directed towards religious conversion. It may be asked whether this pattern was a spontaneous growth in American Protestantism of that time or whether it follows a pattern found in other religious settings. Davenport has suggested that these camp-meetings are closely related to the methods of two American Indian religious movements.[7] These are the Shaker religion of the Indians of Puget Sound and the Ghost-dance religion. In these, as in the Kentucky camp-meetings, cataleptic and convulsive phenomena were produced by mass suggestion, with the medicine-men playing the same part as that of the camp-meeting preachers. Communion with the spirit world was experienced during trances, and, as has been reported of various revival meetings, those unsympathetic to the movement found themselves unable to resist its influence on them. As in the camp-meetings, it appears that these morbid phenomena were accompanied by real improvements in behaviour, and the affected Indians made an attack on their social vices of drinking and gambling.

Although moral advances may sometimes result from such activities as religious revival under conditions of heightened suggestibility, one must also consider the price paid. This involves not only the pathological physical symptoms already described but also a general weakening of the barriers against outside influence on behaviour. Outbreaks of sexual misbehaviour were reported at the Kentucky camp-meetings, and similar reports have been made in other revivals. These charges were not made by opponents of the camp-meetings but by ministers taking part in them. Such loosening of moral controls may be regarded as a secondary consequence of the enhancement of suggestibility resulting from its exploitation for what seem to be good ends.

There is indeed a general ethical question raised by the use of suggestion for religious teaching. If it is possible to change people's opinions simply by confident reiteration, has the religious teacher any right to do so? It may be argued that, in a great deal of teaching, in school and even in the university class-room, the teacher is using non-rational processes of communication. Certainly the school or university teacher regards it as his aim to train his students to think for themselves. He tries to help them to understand both sides of a controversial situation but, so far as he is communicating to them his own opinions (as he often is) he is likely to be using the non-rational method of suggestion, by confident (perhaps repeated) affirmation. The listeners are, of course, not in the hypnoidal state; the teacher hopes that they are intellectually alert and active. His aim, however, is different from that of the religious teacher. The latter may well feel that the attitude of intelligent and critical interest which a science teacher may wish to induce in his pupils is not of much value in religious teaching. He may feel that faith rather than critical awareness is what he is concerned to induce, and that, for this purpose, confident affirmation is a more effective instrument than reasoned demonstration. But confident affirmation can be used to induce a false belief as well as a true, and to use suggestion techniques under conditions of heightened suggestibility as a method of inducing belief imposes on the speaker a grave moral responsibility for ensuring that what he teaches is true. Can he ever be sure enough about this to be justified in using techniques of automatic belief enforcement? It is true that in the passage from Spurgeon quoted above the speaker was using repeated affirmation not to induce belief but to encourage action (preaching) of a type whose value is already taken for granted by the hearers. This is a different use of suggestion, less open to the objections against it as a method of inducing belief.

There are other objections to too great reliance on suggestion in religious teaching. If successful, it may lead to an attitude of dependence on the religious teacher. Such an attitude of dependence with respect to a psychoanalyst has been called by Freud the *positive transference*. The object of the transference takes the place of the earlier authoritative parents and may be the recipient of a dependent and infantile form of affection. When such a transference develops with a minister of religion as its object, the situation created may be difficult for the minister and may react unfavourably on the spiritual growth of the person who has developed it.

A more serious objection to the excessive use of suggestion techniques as a pastoral method is that it may lead to over-valuation of the attitude of passive acceptance of authority. This danger is illustrated by the story of Mr Brownlow North and the sceptical young man referred to earlier. When the young man asked the very reasonable question of why God permitted sin in the world, he was told that if he went on questioning God's dealings, God would send him to hell. The young man is said to have accepted this and to have become happy by deciding to judge things by God's word and not by his own reason. One may, however, question whether such passive acceptance of authority is a satisfactory kind of religious adjustment. Must not the individual's own creative intellectual activities be allowed to interact with what he is taught if his conformity is to be more than superficial? We may notice that Dame Julian of Norwich also asked why sin was not letted, and deepened her religious insights by discussing this question.[9] Would it not have been better for Mr North's young man if he too had been helped to consider this question fruitfully instead of being frightened off it by threats of hell?

## REFERENCES

1. C. S. Isaacson, *Stories of grace*, London, 1908
2. R. A. Torrey, *How to promote and conduct a successful revival*, London, 1901.
3. A. T. Fryer, 'Psychological aspects of the Welsh revival', *Proc. of the Society for Psychical Research*, XIX, London, 1907, pp. 80–161.
4. G. LeBon, *The crowd; a study of the popular mind*, (Eng. trans.), London, 1921.
5. W. Trotter, *Instincts of the herd in peace and war*, London, 1916.
6. J. B. Pratt, *The religious consciousness*, New York, 1920.
7. F. M. Davenport, *Primitive traits in religious revivals*, New York, 1905.
8. J. Wesley, *The journal of John Wesley*, London, 1827.
9. Dame Julian, *Revelations of divine love*, (Ed. Grace Warrack), London, 1901.

# 5. The natural factor in religion

It was suggested earlier that there are three kinds of experience which might be included among the factors which contribute to the religious attitude: the experience of the natural world, of moral conflict, and of certain emotional states that seem to have a religious reference. The suggestion that experiences of these kinds may contribute to the religious attitude, does not mean that they provide intellectual support for religious belief. Rather it is supposed that a man's experiences of the natural world and of his moral conflicts may lead him, in an intuitive and non-verbal way, to a feeling that both the natural world and the system of moral demands are expressions of a spiritual world, and are therefore of religious significance. If his religious attitude is of a theistic type, he may express this feeling by saying, for example, that the natural world is a manifestation of God, and that the demands of morality are the requirements of God's will. Later, the holder of a religious belief may have to defend it, and he may then use some argument based on his experience of the natural world, such as the argument from design as developed by Paley.[1] But, it is not as such an intellectual process that the contribution of experience of the natural world to the religious attitude may be supposed to start. It is not that a man experiences the world and argues that it must have a creator; rather, he begins by experiencing the world as something having a God-like, or at least a supernatural stamp, and later replaces this intuition by a verbal argument. The effect of the argument may be to strengthen the religious conviction originally based on intuition. On the other hand, later intellection may weaken or destroy the conviction that the religious interpretation is the right one, since, on critical examination, the appearance of design may be judged to be illusory.

The raw experience, not intellectualised or worked into an argument, has been frequently described in literature. A well-known example is to be found in the chapter on solitude in Thoreau's *Walden*:

I was suddenly sensible of such sweet and beneficent society in Nature, in the very pattering of the drops, and in every sight and sound around my house, an infinite and unaccountable friendliness all at once like an atmosphere sustaining me, as made the fancied advantages of human neighbourhood insignificant, and I have never thought of them since. Every little pine-needle expanded and swelled with sympathy and befriended me. I was so distinctly made aware of something kindred to me even in scenes which we are accustomed to call wild and dreary ... that I thought no place could ever be strange to me again.[2]

This passage seems to describe a religious experience in the sense in which 'religious' was defined in Chapter 2 although it contains no reference to God. It describes, without interpreting, an experience which might easily have been described in theistic terms. That indeed is how one would expect such an experience to be described by someone with a theistic background. The following, for example, is the narrative of the beginning of a man's religious life.

I was living in a small town in one of the southern counties of England, and one Sunday afternoon I went out into the country for a stroll. It was summer, and after walking for a few miles I lay down on the side of a hill. I saw, stretching to the distant horizon, meadows and orchards and cornfields; the cloudless skies were gloriously blue, and the sun was flooding earth and heaven with splendour. The wonderful beauty filled me with excitement and delight. And then suddenly, through all that I saw, there came the very glory of God. I knew that He was there. His presence, His power, and His goodness took possession of me and held me for hours.[3]

Such interpretation may be regarded as a result of the fact that the experience in question does not act alone; it interacts with all other facts determining the religious attitude, including the religious tradition that has been acquired from other people. If the natural factor acted alone or predominantly, it might be expected to produce a religious attitude of a pantheistic type in which God was regarded as immanent and not as also transcendent – in every-day language as 'here' and in no sense as 'out there'. If, however, the element of transcendence is supplied by other factors, this kind of experience may make its contribution to the type of theism which is found in the Jewish, Christian and Islamic traditions.

While such experiences are commonly interpreted theistically by those living within a theistic tradition, it does not seem that this interpretation necessarily belongs to the experience. Similar experiences may be reported by those who do not interpret them theistically. An example is to be found in Swinburne's poem *A Nympholept*:

The whole wood feels thee, the whole air fears thee; but fear
So deep, so dim, so sacred, is wellnigh sweet.

For the light that hangs and broods on the woodlands here,
Intense, invasive, intolerant, imperious, and meet
To lighten the works of thine hands and the ways of thy feet,
Is hot with the fire of the breath of thy life, and dear
As hope that shrivels and shrinks not for frost or heat.

This passage is like the others in describing an emotional relationship to natural objects similar to that which might be felt towards a
person. The natural world is not treated as a mere collection of
non-sentient objects, but as something with which the observer may
have personal relations, for. which he may feel love and awe. Yet
Swinburne was not a theist; he would not be inclined to say that his
poem was describing the experience of the presence of God in a wood.
The raw material for a theistic interpretation was present, but other
elements necessary for building up a theistic religious attitude must
have been absent from Swinburne's experience. He found Nature
beautiful without finding in it, or elsewhere, evidence of the goodness
which would be necessary to a full theistic experience.

Three elements may perhaps be distinguished in the contributions
of the experience of the external world to the religious attitude: the
experiences of beneficence, of harmony and of beauty.

The experience of beneficence arises from the fact that some things
in Nature are regarded as favourable to man: gentle warmth, season-
able rains, fertile crops and domestic animals, and all those events
which preserve his life and promote his well-being. Others are
regarded as unfavourable to him: extremes of heat and cold, tempests,
insect pests, wild beasts, diseases and all uncomfortable or disastrous
happenings. If he sees in the former the works of a divine being or of
divine beings who love him, and in the latter the activity of a being
who is hostile to him, he has the raw material for a very simple
religion. If this were all that entered into the religious attitude, it
would give an anthropocentric and dualistic religion. There is probably no religion, however primitive, in which this is the sole element,
in which the object of religion is simply that of being a means of
satisfying human needs and wishes. At the same time, this, which may
be called the *providence* factor, is present as an element in all religions,
at any rate until a high level of mysticism is reached. At that level, it
may appear to be abandoned as when St Catherine of Genoa
exclaimed: 'I will not name myself either for good or for evil, lest this
my (selfish) part should esteem itself to be something.'[4] Few religious
individuals would go as far as St Catherine in this matter. A view of
God which exaggerates the role of providence as concern for our
personal welfare may be considered a primitive and infantile one; God
must be to the mature faith more than a universal provider. Yet this
conception may be one of the strands that make up a mature religious
faith. The behavioural correlate of the conception of God as

providence is the practice of petitionary prayer, the problems of which will be discussed in a later chapter.

There is more in the contribution of the experience of the external world to the religious attitude than the concept of God as provider for human needs. There is also the fact that a man may see in that world a harmony and purpose which has nothing to do with the satisfying of human requirements. What is meant by the experience of harmony and purpose may be illustrated by reference to Paley's *Natural theology*.[1] Paley argued from the mutual adaptations of the parts of organisms and from the adaptation of organisms to their environment that they were created by a personal designer. He may have been wrong on the logical point that this argument proves the reality of a personal designer but right on the psychological point that this is one of the reasons men believe in a personal designer. If this is the case, we may say that this kind of experience, in which the world seems to have the character of a manufactured article, is one of the roots of the religious attitude.

Thirdly, there is the experience of beauty in the world. This is, no doubt, not an important element in the experience of many people. There are some, however, to whom the world appears wonderfully and inexplicably beautiful. They do not feel, with Paley, that the world is like a watch; it seems to them rather to be like a picture. This too implies that they are inclined to regard it as made by someone, and even by an artist whose purpose they can to some degree penetrate. There are many expressions in prose and poetry of this sense of the beauty of the world revealing a spiritual world or, more specifically, revealing an aspect of God. An example has already been given earlier in this chapter and Gerard Manley Hopkins may have referred to a similar experience when he said:

> The world is charged with the grandeur of God.
> It will flame out, like shining from shook foil.[5]

The experience of beauty has been intellectualised into a philosophical argument that the presence of beauty in the world implies a creator of that beauty. This may be called the *aesthetic* argument for the existence of God. As with Paley's argument from design, the psychologist is not concerned with the validity of the aesthetic argument. He may, however, regard the appeal to this argument as confirmation of the hypothesis that the experience of beauty is one factor in the production of a religious attitude.

Whether or not the passage from the experiences of beneficence, harmony and beauty in the natural world to religious belief can be rationally justified as valid, this passage would seem to be a natural psychological process. If things in the world seem to anyone to be, on the whole, arranged so as to be favourable to his own needs and those of other men, it is understandable that he should come to believe that the natural order is under the control of someone who is taking care of him. If the world seems, on the whole, to be ordered on an intelligible plan, it is understandable that a man may infer that there is an intelligent designer of the world. If the world seems to him to be beautiful, it is understandable that he may regard this beauty as the expression of a personal designer. The belief in God may then be regarded as an intellectualisation of the experience.

An important psychological characteristic of the kind of theistic religion derived from these experiences results from the fact that the conception of God to which it leads is one that regards part of the totality of experience as hostile to his nature. This rejected part of experience consists of the elements of malevolence, disorder and ugliness. By malevolence is meant everything in nature that is opposed to man's well-being: famine, extremes of heat and cold, illness and death. These form part of the experience of the average man and are a predominant part of the experience of some. By disorder is meant all those natural events which seem to show an absence of design. The fate of individuals seems often to be capricious and to be unrelated to their merit. One animal preys on another. The end situation of the world to which science points seems to be one of lifelessness and meaninglessness. There are elements in the world which give an immediate impression of evil design; a limbless parasite, living on the blood of its host, may show the same exact adaptation to its environment as do the higher animals whose adaptations seemed so admirable to eighteenth-century religious apologists. Man too has a darker side to his evolutionary history in his increased capacity to suffer pain and to inflict pain and destruction on other organisms. Such facts give a total picture of waste and disorder at least as impressive as the world of design depicted by Paley. Finally, in opposition to the experience of beauty, there is the equally real experience of ugliness in the many aspects of the world which seem to the observer to be sordid, unlovely, or revolting.

Religious thought, so far as it is derived from experiences of the natural world, is likely to contain an element of dualism, contrasting beneficence–malevolence, harmony–disorder, beauty–ugliness, good–evil. This tendency to dualism may indeed be modified by other factors, including reflective thought. It may be expressed by a system of belief which opposes a real (perhaps personal) power of evil against the powers of good. This power of evil may be regarded as one that is ultimately to be overcome, indeed that is a necessary part of a belief system in an optimistic religious attitude, but the grounds for such optimism are not provided by the experience of the natural world.

There is another way in which this darker side of the experienced world may be dealt with in a religious system; it may be regarded as part of the divine nature which includes the forces of destruction and disorder as well as those of creation and order. This is found in Hindu thought though it appears strange to those whose religious ideas come through the Jewish–Christian tradition. Thus, in the *Gita*, Arjuna is reported to have seen Krishna in his divine character; this vision showed not only glory and love but also terror and destruction.

> When I see you, Vishnu, omnipresent,
> Shouldering the sky, in hues of rainbow,
> With your mouths agape and flame-eyes staring –
> All my peace is gone; my heart is troubled.
>
> Now with frightful tusks your mouths are gnashing,
> Flaring like the fires of Doomsday morning –
> North, south, east and west seem all confounded –
> Lord of devas, world's abode, have mercy![6]

There is still another way in which that part of the experience of the natural world that includes the elements of malevolence, disorder and ugliness may play a part in determining the belief system belonging to the religious attitude. It may be regarded as neither foundation for belief in a power of evil opposed to God nor as itself the dark side of God; it may provide instead the raw material for an atheistic and pessimistic interpretation of the world. Hardy, in his novels, gave a picture of a fate indifferent to human happiness and to the merits of individuals, capriciously crushing and destroying his finest characters. He ironically referred to this as the sport of the President of the Immortals. To him malevolence and disorder were facts too salient in the experience of the world to admit the possibility of its interpretation in terms of a benevolent God.

The most influential example of this negative attitude towards the experience of nature is to be found in the teaching of the Buddha. We are told that Gotama Buddha lived through a protected childhood in his father's palace in which it was intended that he should be guarded from experience of the negative aspects of the world. As a young man, however, he met with examples of disease, old age and death. These seemed to him, afterwards, to be the predominant facts of the world and he devoted his life to the quest for a means of escape from suffering. This led him to a solution that involved a pessimistic attitude towards the world and a religion that was effectively atheistic, not in the sense that it denied the existence of gods or of the supreme God, but that it denied their power to help. The follower of the Buddha was taught not to trust to God but to his own efforts for the achievement of salvation. The first step in this achievement was to understand the nature of the world process as expressed in the four noble truths which dealt with the nature of suffering and the means of escape from suffering.[7]

The negative elements in the experience of nature do not necessarily produce any of these adjustments of the religious belief system which range from dualism to atheism. Perhaps for most religious believers they provide a point of tension within their religious belief system. There are various ways in which this tension may be partially or wholly relieved. It may, on the other hand, be ignored when a religious faith is built up from consideration of the more pleasant aspect of the world while its more sinister aspects are disregarded. Such a faith is obviously built on insecure foundations. Yet it must be noticed that the natural factor in religion has been strong in many of those who have not closed their eyes to the unpleasant aspects of the world. To St Francis, for example, the world appeared to be full of God although he deliberately put himself in contact with some of its very unpleasant aspects.

## REFERENCES

1. W. Paley, *Natural theology*, London, 1802.
2. H. D. Thoreau, *Walden*, Edinburgh, 1884.
3. R. W. Dale, *Christian doctrine*, London, 1894.
4. F. von Hügel, *The mystical element of religion*, London, 1909.
5. G. M. Hopkins, 'God's Grandeur', *Poems*, London, 1918.
6. Isherwood and Prabhavananda (Trans.), *The song of God: Bhagavad-Gita*, London, 1947.
7. T. W. Rhys Davids, (Trans.), 'The foundation of the kingdom of righteousness', *Sacred books of the East*, XI, Oxford,1881.

# 6. The moral conflict

The last chapter dealt with experiences of the outside world which may contribute to the formation of a religious attitude. The present chapter is concerned with an experience more internal to the individual himself, that of the conflict between some of his own behaviour tendencies and an opposing system of requirements of which he recognises the authority. This system of requirements is commonly called the *moral law*; the psychological conflict which arises from it may be called the *moral conflict*.

The psychologist is not concerned with philosophical problems concerning the nature of the obligations imposed by the moral law. Various possible answers to this question have been put forward. The moral law may be considered to be a system of social requirements developed by a community and transmitted to successive generations by a process of social conditioning. It may, on the other hand, be regarded as a system of obligations which would be binding on man whether or not they were socially useful. It has been claimed by some that these obligations are known intuitively; others have supposed that they can be deduced by processes of reasoning, others have regarded them as having been supernaturally revealed. Whatever may be the answers to these ethical questions, the point of importance for the psychologist is that the moral conflict is a real psychological fact. However the division between right and wrong may have originated, the distinction between them is a real part of the individual's experience. One way in which this reality is shown is that he tends to develop a feeling of guilt when he has behaved in a way which his social training had led him to regard as wrong behaviour. It seems clear that the moral conflict is not itself a product of the religious attitude; those who have no religious faith or who have lost their religious faith may be as much under the influence of a system of moral obligations as those with a strongly developed religious attitude. Indeed the contents of this system of obligations may be much the same for the religious and the irreligious. Yet there are important psychological interactions between the religious attitude and the moral conflict. It is here suggested that among these interactions is the tendency of the experience of the moral conflict to provide one of the roots of the religious attitude.

The moral conflict may be considered to be a factor in determining the religious attitude in much the same way as is the experience of nature. The conflict is experienced as one between the good and the evil forces in one's own self. The forces for good may be explained as those on the side of some good being or beings, the forces for evil as those on the opposite side. These forces for evil may also be personified, as belonging to an evil being or beings. Thus the belief in a good God may be regarded as, in part, an intellectualisation of the moral conflict. This intellectualisation is given the form of a demonstrative argument in the *moral argument* for the existence of God. If it is agreed that the demands of morality are real and objective, it is argued that this reality can only be accounted for by postulating the existence of God. As psychologists, we are not concerned with the validity of this argument. The fact that it has been put forward, however, suggests the psychological hypothesis that this is one of the factors in the creation of a religious attitude.

This moral factor is like the natural factor in that its obvious tendency is to produce a religious attitude of a dualistic type. There is, opposed to the realm of God and goodness, another realm, of evil, which may also be regarded as having a personal controller or devil. In this case also, the dualism may be more or less modified in particular religious traditions, but, so far as it is derived from the experience of the moral conflict, an element of dualism remains in the Christian religion. There is a realm of evil opposed to God, and although evil may be regarded as a deprivation of good, this does not deny the reality of evil; cold is a deprivation of heat, but this does not make coldness any less real than hotness. This element of dualism remains a region of tension within the religious tradition containing it. Many religious persons have been led to ask with Dame Julian of Norwich why 'sin was not letted'.[1]

It is an essential of an optimistic religion that it should contain the hope that, in the end, this dualism will be resolved, although it may not describe clearly how this will happen. It is said, for example, that the Zarathustrian religion (generally condemned as excessively dualistic) taught that: 'finally the powers of good and evil will engage in a last conflict. Ahriman and the evil host will be cast into the stream of molten metal. Then will the whole world be purified, the whole universe filled with Ahura Mazda's being, and all that lives will pass into immortality and celestial perfection.'[2] This hope may be paralleled in the Christian tradition by Dame Julian's real but indefinite assurance that 'all shall be well, and all shall be well, and all manner of thing shall be well.'[1]

This is not, however, the only way in which the moral conflict contributes to the religious attitude. Some people seem to pass from the moral conflict to a belief in God by the practical need which they feel for this belief if they are to be adequately motivated to right conduct. They feel that without religious belief they would not be kept good at all. If they give a correct account of the process, they are suggesting that their religious belief is not the intellectualisation of their moral experience but a belief dictated by a practical need. It is a recognised psychological fact that if an individual feels a strong practical need for a belief to be true, he is inclined automatically to accept that belief as true. This is a process which has been called *wish-fulfilment*. It may not, of course, be the sole ground for the acceptance of a particular belief; it may merely make it easier to accept a belief which has other origins.

An individual's opinion that he needs his religion to keep him good may be an illusory one. It may be true that his motivation towards good behaviour is largely derived from within his religious attitude, but this does not preclude the possibility that if he lost or changed his religious attitude, he might find an effective motivation in some other system of ideas. The resultant behaviour might not be exactly the same as before but it would be unlikely to differ so much that outside observers would be inclined to say that he was formerly a good man but was now a wicked one. This general tendency to conservation of patterns of behaviour under changing systems of ideas is, no doubt, partly due to the fact that different systems of ideas may provide effective motivation for similar behaviour patterns, partly to the fact that accepted behaviour patterns depend not only on our systems of ideas, but also on our inherited and acquired qualities of character which may not change with a change of our attitude towards religion. This is not to deny that an individual's religious attitude may react with his moral ideas and with his patterns of behaviour in many ways. Religious ideas may provide motives for humility and for loving self-sacrifice that are more effective than those provided by other systems of ideas. If we hear that a man has thrown up a well-paid position in a business in order that he may take a subordinate job in a leper hospital, we cannot be certain that he is a religious man acting from religious motives but there is a very high probability that he is. Religious conversion may also be accompanied by dramatic character changes for the better; drunkards may change to sober and useful citizens and drug addicts may lose their addiction.[3] It may well be the case that other sudden changes of attitude (such as political re-orientations) may produce dramatic changes of character but there seems to be much evidence that the religious re-orientation is particularly effective in doing so.

There is an opinion held by many at the present day that the promotion of good conduct is the proper function of religion and that everything not concerned with this end is an accretion that should be eliminated from an adequate modern religion. It is no part of the task of the psychologist to pronounce on the proper aim of religion, but we may note that this view of its function is not the traditional view of any religion. The Buddha taught that the end of his way of life was the final escape from sorrow and that right conduct was one of the means to that end. Christians have regarded the love of God as the supreme aim, and have valued good conduct as a means of achieving that end.

The problem has practical importance in connection with religious education. It is often suggested that juvenile delinquency is the result of inadequate religious teaching and that religious teachers should regard it as their aim to eliminate delinquency in their pupils. Religious teaching directed towards the development of religious faith may, if it is effectively carried out, have many effects on pupil's behaviour. Its effect on the problem of juvenile delinquency may, nevertheless, remain disappointing, partly because those prone to delinquency are likely to be impervious to religious teaching, partly because such effects on behaviour as are to be observed are likely to be mainly in other directions than that of increasing conformity to commonly accepted standards of conduct. Above all, the effects may be expected to be disappointing if the teaching is carried out by those convinced that the religious attitude is not an end in itself but a device for securing conformity to moral standards.

An early experimental research into religious education was concerned with the problem of how far the amount of a child's Biblical information was related to the development of desirable traits of character. Dr Hightower reported in 1921 a research in which over 3,000 American school children were given a test for the amount of their biblical information and another test for the presence of such desirable character traits as honesty and loyalty.[4] No correlation was found between the results of the two tests; mere biblical information seemed to have no measurable influence on these character traits. If one object of teaching Scripture is to increase the honesty of the children studying it, this aim appears not to have been attained in the group investigated by Dr Hightower. For interpretation of this result, however, one should also know how Scripture was taught. Psychological research on the transfer of training would lead us to expect that increased honesty would not follow automatically from learning by heart the routes of the missionary journeys of St Paul any more than it would from learning the multiplication table. It would be rash to conclude that religious education has no effect on character; its effects are likely to depend to a large extent on how far the moral effect is specifically aimed at in the teaching. It obviously does not provide the only educational vehicle for moral teaching; honesty and self-sacrifice may be taught in lessons on mathematics or history but there may be real advantages in religious education for this purpose, and certain virtues may be more easily motivated in a religious lesson than elsewhere. The demonstration of such differential effects would, however, require an experiment of much more complex design than has hitherto been used, with measurement of various directions of moral improvement and careful control of methods of teaching the topics under investigation. Such investigations in religious education have not, so far as I know, been carried out.

Another line of psychological investigation of religious education has comprised a number of investigations of children's responses to such ideas as that 'good people go to heaven and bad people go to hell'.[5] The general finding is that, with increasing age, there is a rapidly decreasing number of children who assent to such statements. One obviously cannot conclude that the force of religious moral sanctions declines as the children grow older. The only reliable conclusion would seem to be that if children are presented with crude religious ideas, they are more likely to accept them at an early age than they are later. It may, of course, be reasonably doubted whether such presentation at an early age is providing a useful foundation for mature religious ideas or for mature moral motivation.

An apparent point of conflict between the religious and the psychological point of view is the valuation of a consciousness of one's own sinfulness. Many religious writers in the Christian tradition have written as if the sense of sin were of such value that it could not be too strongly intensified. On the other hand, writers on psychotherapy, especially those following the psychoanalytic tradition, have written as if the sense of guilt were a pathological symptom to be got rid of by suitable psychotherapeutic measures. The conflict is perhaps more apparent than real. Guilt feelings are unpleasant but serviceable: they produce negative reinforcement of the lines of conduct producing them and consequent lower probability of those lines of conduct being followed again. So far, they are useful as serving moral ends. They become pathological, however, when they are attached to indifferent lines of behaviour (as in scrupulosity), when they are free-floating and attached to no particular behaviour, and, finally, when they are of such great strength that they are no longer effective incentives to right conduct.

Bunyan is an example of an individual in whom the sense of guilt reached such an intensity that one is led to ask whether it was of moral value to him or whether it should be regarded as a psychopathological symptom. He tells the story vividly in his own book *Grace abounding*.[6] From his childhood, he said, he had few equals for cursing, lying and blaspheming. He was frightened, however, by fearful dreams and by apprehensions of hell fire. After his marriage, he began to go to church, but the thought of the grievousness of his many sins made his heart sink in despair, for he was convinced that it was too late for him to hope for forgiveness. Later, he reformed his words and life, and his neighbours began to take him for a very godly man, although he said that in reality he knew neither Christ, nor grace, nor faith, nor hope. Now he had great peace in his conscience and thought God must be pleased with him. However, when he heard some poor women at Bedford talking about religion and speaking of a new birth and of the filthiness and insufficiency of their own right-eousness, his heart began to shake. He became doubtful as to whether or not he had *faith*. For years, he alternated between depressed and elated conditions, with depression predominating. Troubled, and tossed, and afflicted with the sense of his own wickedness; he was also afraid that this trouble might pass away from him and that he might lose his sense of guilt without remission of his sins. He then became convinced that he had committed the unforgiveable sin by consenting in thought to the selling of Christ.* For two years nothing could occupy his mind but damnation and the expectation of damnation. In the end a study of Scripture convinced him that he had not commited the sin against the Holy Ghost, and that salvation came by the righteousness of Christ. After this time, comfort and peace were his usual state, and the periods of depression were only occasional.

One psychologist has judged Bunyan's struggles to be altogether without moral significance.[7] This is perhaps too superficial. Bunyan may have been right in his conviction that his first contentment with his own righteousness was an attitude that fell short of spiritual maturity. The agonies of his later struggles of conscience may have been to some degree pathological and yet have been a road to spiritual growth. Spiritual growth may be achieved in some people through the agonies of an undoubtedly pathological physical illness; in others it may be achieved through a pathological mental condition. Bunyan did emerge from his obsessions of guilt to write *The Pilgrim's Progress*. Other weaker souls may never emerge from similar cycles of ideas of guilt; the achievement of Bunyan is not sufficient ground for regarding an intensified sense of guilt as a normal or desirable element in spiritual development.

In extreme contrast to Bunyan, whose sense of guilt seems often to have been too strong to be serviceable to his moral life, we may turn to the case of Benvenuto Cellini whose autobiography reveals a personality with a pathologically under-developed sense of guilt.[8] Cellini was a great artist, but his life contained a series of dis-creditable episodes for which he seemed to feel no remorse. He was devout and lived in an atmosphere of intense religious emotion, yet he seemed to feel no inconsistency in the fact that his life was one of profligacy and murder. While leaving Mass full of religious feelings, he murdered an enemy in cold blood. Thrown into prison, he was

* A not uncommon obsession amongst depressed persons whose guilt feelings become attached to religious ideas. It is based on the passage in St Mark's gospel (3.29): whoever blasphemes against the Holy Spirit never has forgiveness but is guilty of an eternal sin. The power of this passage to provide material for a guilt obsession is, no doubt, enhanced by uncertainty about the exact nature of the sin referred to.

supported by a sense of the divine favour and he claimed that afterwards he had an aureole of glory on his head.

A practical problem for religious bodies is the necessity for avoiding both of these extremes. If the sense of guilt for real wrong-doing is too much reduced, there is a lack of motivation for resisting impulses to wrong-doing. The solution is not, however, a mere intensification of the sense of guilt; that too may lead to a lack of useful correlation between wrongness of conduct and degree of guilt feeling. Religious bodies should aim at keeping their followers from becoming Cellinis without turning them into Bunyans. Awareness of the darker side of one's own nature is as necessary for good living as it is for mental health, yet there must also be found a way of dealing with this darker side which prevents it from becoming a frightening burden.

One of the ways that religious bodies have developed of dealing with this problem is the practice of the confession of sins. This has been most systematised in the Roman Catholic and Greek Orthodox churches where confession is made regularly to a priest, although the practice of making confessions of sin before other persons is found also in many Protestant bodies. We are not concerned with the sacramental aspects of this practice but only with its psychological effects. Ideally it would seem to be a way in which the individual is compelled to face his darker side by confession of his wrong-doings, while he is enabled to come to terms with it by the authoritative assurance of forgiveness which is conveyed by the priest's absolution. Dr Janet (himself an agnostic) claimed that confession to a priest was of value in releasing psycho-neurotic individuals from their scruples. He said, indeed that regular confession seems to have been invented by an alienist of genius who wished to treat obsessed patients.[9] He said that he had himself sent patients to priests who fulfilled the required role perfectly, although others were so ignorant and tactless that the work of direction must fall on the physician.

If ideally the psychological value of confession to a priest is that, while providing a disciplinary remedy against sin, it also maintains a healthy-minded attitude towards it, this ideal may not always be achieved in practice. Regular confession and absolution may result in its practitioners tending to reduce right living to conformity to a system of rules, often of a trivial kind, and deflect attention from the real problems of moral and spiritual growth. Many moral theologians are now concerned with the question of how far this is currently happening and how the practice of confession might be so modified as to increase its psychotherapeutic value. It would be an interesting topic for research to discover how far those who regularly practice confession to a priest have a lower incidence of guilt obsessions than those who do not. Since there does not seem to be any research directed towards discovering this, opinions as to the therapeutic value of the practice of confession remain somewhat speculative.

It may seem paradoxical to suggest that the feeling of guilt may reach such intensity that it ceases to be an effective incentive to morality. It might be supposed that, if the effect of feeling guilty is to discourage wrong behaviour, then the strengthening of the sense of guilt must always have the effect of increasing the forces driving the individual towards right lines of conduct. This, however, is not necessarily the case. An emotion driving towards a particular line of conduct may have an optimal strength; if it develops beyond this optimal point it may become increasingly ineffective. This may be illustrated by the example of fear; if fear is developed to a moderate strength it drives the organism to escape from danger, but if developed to very high intensity, it may make escape more difficult, since muscular effort may become impossible and the organism may collapse in the face of danger. That this may be the case with the sense of guilt was recognised long before the development of modern psychology. In the stories of the Fathers who lived in the Egyptian desert, it is told that one Father consulted the blessed man Pachomius about his temptations which were so violent that he felt disposed to give up the life of the desert and return to the world.[10] Pachomius replied that this temptation had fallen upon the other as a result of his strenuousness, and described how he had himself spent long years struggling against similar temptations, until he became convinced that the temptations were sent to him to deliver him from excessive self-confidence. Then he ceased to have anxious care about them, and continued in peace from this struggle to the end of his days; this particular devil, seeing that he had stopped worrying about the matter, never approached him again.

It is interesting to find a similar prescription of relaxation of effort in the early history of Buddhism. It is recorded of Sāriputta, one of the immediate disciples of the Buddha, that he was approached for spiritual advice by one Anuruddha, who reported that, in spite of his spiritual attainments in the direction of mindfulness, bodily tranquillity and concentration, he still found that his mind was not free from the evil of attachment.[11]

It is related that Sāriputta pointed out to him that his satisfaction with his spiritual attainments was conceit and that his anxiety about his remaining imperfections was worry, and that it would be good if he abandoned both conceit and worry, paying no further attention to them. By taking this advice, Anuruddha is said to have achieved the aim of enlightenment and detachment.

The advice to relax effort against sin does not, of course, imply the general principle that the remedy for sin is to lose one's sense of guilt and to relax effort towards right conduct. It is rather to be supposed that the adviser recognised that there is an optimal intensity of direct effort and that, in these cases, it had been exceeded. The point is that those concerned with the task of advising on moral problems should know when their task is that of increasing guilt feelings and intensifying effort towards the good life and when it is that of reducing guilt and encouraging the relaxation of effort. Pastors have perhaps traditionally regarded themselves as primarily concerned with the former problem and have had too little awareness of the other. Secular psychotherapists, on the other hand, have been more concerned with the reduction of guilt feelings and the relaxation of effort, for the obvious reason that this is more likely to fulfil the needs of their neurotic patients.

Finally, there are other disturbed individuals, such as delinquents, whose problems are the opposite ones; they behave very badly and there is no correcting factor to their bad behaviour arising from any sense of guilt about it. These too are in need of psychological treatment whether their cure is in the hands of a pastor or a psychotherapist. Neither may know how to give them such a sense of guilt about their bad behaviour as to motivate improvement. How this may best be done is a problem for future psychological research.

## REFERENCES

1. Dame Julian, *Revelations of divine love*, (ed. Grace Warrack), London, 1901.
2. F. B. Jevon, *Comparative religion*, Cambridge, 1913.
3. D. Wilkerson, *The cross and the switchblade*, Westwood (N.J.), 1962.
4. P. T. Hightower, 'Biblical information in relation to character and conduct', *Proc. 9th International Congress of Psychology*, Princeton (N.J.), 1930.
5. F. Hilliard, 'The influence of religious education upon the development of children's moral ideas', *British Journal of Educational Psychology*, 19, 1959, pp. 50–9.
6. John Bunyan, *Grace abounding to the chief of sinners*, London, 1666.
7. J. B. Pratt, *The religious consciousness*, New York, 1920.
8. Benvenuto Cellini, *Life* (trans. J. A. Symonds), London, 1888.
9. P. Janet, *Les Obsessions et la psychasthénie*, Paris, 1908.
10. E. A. T. W. Budge, *The paradise or garden of the Holy Fathers*, London, 1907.
11. Thera Nyanoponika, *The life of Sāriputta*, Kandy, 1966.

# 7. The emotional factor in religion

It was suggested earlier that one of the factors contributing to the religious attitude was the system of emotional experiences which people have in connection with their religion. This may be called the 'emotional' or the 'affective' factor in the religious attitude. It has been called the 'mystical' element in religion but, although there is no coercive reason against using the word 'mystical' in this sense, it seems better to reserve it for the more dramatic experiences of the unusual individuals commonly classified as religious mystics. It is true that no sharp line can be drawn between these two types of religious experience. Every religious person has a certain amount of emotional experience in connection with his religion; it may even be intense without differing in kind from the religious experiences of the majority of other people. In some individuals, however, there occur religious experiences of unusual strength and constancy which seem to differ markedly from those of other people. These are the individuals commonly called *mystics* who will be discussed in Chapter 15.

When we talk of religious experiences we may mean a kind of experience that can also occur originally in a non-religious setting but is inclined to result in the development of religious belief, or we may mean a type of experience that arises during religious behaviour and may confirm, enrich, or otherwise modify previously held beliefs. The emotional experiences connected with the beauty of nature which were discussed in Chapter 5 show the first type, for example, Thoreau's description of a feeling of a prevailing friendliness in the sights and sounds around his lonely dwelling. Such descriptions often report a sense of an intimate pervading presence and of a deeper significance in surrounding things and in one's own life, and sometimes also some degree of loss of personal identity which may reflect a deep absorption in the experience. The individual may interpret his feeling theistically and say, for example, that he has 'enjoyed communication with God', but the experience does not preclude a different explanation. Some people will reject a theistic interpretation on intellectual grounds, others as a result of contradictory experiences.

The feeling of being in direct contact with supernatural realities may also be brought about by the action of certain drugs. One of the earliest of these to receive experimental study was nitrous oxide (laughing gas). This was being actively investigated towards the end of the last century, and a vivid account of the matter is given by William James in his *Varieties of religious experience*.[1] James himself experimented with it and reported an experience of reconciliation in which all the opposites of the world seemed to be melted into a unity. He was inclined to think that this was not merely an illusion created by the drug but rather an experience of an aspect of reality hidden from our everyday consciousness.

James also reports an experience of J. A. Symonds with chloroform. This occurred during an operation and not as part of a psychological experiment. Symonds describes how, under the anaesthetic, his soul 'became aware of God ... I felt him streaming in like light upon me'. He then describes the horror of his disillusionment as he gradually awoke from the anaesthetic and returned to normal consciousness. 'Only think of it', he wrote, 'To have felt for that long dateless ecstasy of vision the very God, in all purity and tenderness and truth and absolute love, and then to find that I had after all had no revelation, but that I had been tricked by the abnormal excitement of my brain.' It may be that Symonds gave up his vision too easily. If an emotional experience involving a new way of interpreting reality follows the administration of a drug, it does not follow that the experience is illusory and has been created by the drug. It may be that the drug removes temporarily some normal obstacle to perception of a reality.

That a drug may give insight into reality by removing barriers was strongly argued by Aldous Huxley from the experiences he had with mescalin,[2] the drug extracted from peyote (*Lophophora williamsii*), a small spineless cactus found in Mexico. Peyote is eaten (fresh or dried) as the essential rite in the Native American Church.[3] This is a religious organisation found among various Indian tribes in the USA, based on Christianity but adapted to traditional Indian beliefs and practices. In this body, peyote is chewed during a night-long session, after physical and spiritual purification (putting aside evil thoughts, etc.). It is accompanied by prayer and singing, and the emotional experiences which result from the chewing of peyote under these conditions are interpreted as the reception of power from God. Its fruits are said to include not only a rapturous enlightenment, but also the lasting achievement of such virtues as humility, temperance and loving kindness.

Huxley observed that his own taking of mescalin caused an enhanced intensity of visual perception parallel to the spontaneous religious experiences in which the natural world is said to be seen as if new or glorified. He attributes this appearance to the fact that things are seen in their particularity and not, as in normal adult vision, automatically subordinated to the concept. He thought highly of the religious value of this experience of glory and newness in the visible world and referred to it as 'a gratuitous grace, not necessary to salvation but potentially helpful and to be accepted thankfully if made available'.

Mescalin is one of a number of drugs that have amongst their effects the production of an altered state of consciousness in which the drug-taker feels that he perceives a new order of reality. These are now commonly called *psychedelic* (mind-opening) drugs. The nature of their effect on the religious life of the persons taking them can obviously be made the subject of experimental enquiry and such an enquiry has been made by Dr Pahnke.[4] He took as his subjects twenty graduate students with middle-class Protestant backgrounds. Before attending a Good Friday religious service, half of them were given 30 ml of a psychedelic drug (psilocybin) while the other half were used as a control and given an inactive placebo. The religious service occupied two and a half hours and included music, solos, readings, prayers and meditation. Each of the subjects wrote an account of his experiences afterwards, and answered questions on it then and after a period of six months. The conclusion of the experimenter was that those who had received the drug had religious experiences which seemed to him to be indistinguishable from certain of those belonging to mystical consciousness. In all but one of the nine categories of religious experience tested, the experimental group showed significantly higher scores than the control group. This seems to indicate that the use of a drug may measurably enhance religious experiences gained in more conventional ways; it does not suggest that the use of the drug will, in itself, initiate such experiences although this may also be true.

In considering the religious value of the emotional experiences induced by, or enhanced by, certain drugs, one must not lose sight of the fact that habitual dependence on drugs for emotional stimulation can lead to addiction and to physiological and psychological deterioration. It is said that mescalin does not produce addiction and that it has no undesirable side effects. Even so, the individual who has experimented with mescalin may go on to explore the more intense emotional experiences of the more dangerous addictive drugs. It is true that experiences gained from drugs may be felt to give an insight into reality which is of religious value, but it is a dangerous road for a religious institution to encourage its members to follow and it is not surprising that the Native American Church remains alone in adopting this means of attaining religious experience.

There are other practices of religion which have the result of creating emotional experiences in their participants even though this may not be their primary aim. Without any emotional accompaniment the practices of religion would become somewhat empty and formal. An observer of alien religious rites may be tempted to comment: 'This is mere meaningless ceremonial.' His reason for making this judgment may be that he is witnessing these religious practices in their external aspect without himself experiencing the emotional accompaniment which gives them significance to the worshippers. Such a judgment ought not to be made by a psychologist who should understand that to the worshippers themselves there may be no meaningless ceremonial. What appears so to the outside observer may, to the participant, be rich in affective significance. In communal prayer or in the offering of sacrifice, there is likely to be a strong sense of the presence of and of communication with the Divine, and these experiences may be effective in relieving distress and in inducing peace and happiness.

Such emotional experiences may come from religious practices which do not seek principally to arouse an emotional response. There are, however, other religious practices which seem to have as a considerable part of their purpose the intensification of the emotional experiences of the worshippers. This aim is valued differently in different religious traditions, some regarding the worshippers' feelings as of secondary importance, others having the deliberate aim of inducing strong emotion which may be regarded as evidence of the descent of 'the Spirit'. Apart from the rare use of such drugs as peyote, the principal agents inducing emotional experience during religious services would seem to be: ceremonial, music, and emotional oratory.

Religious bodies using an elaborate ceremonial in their worship would not generally regard the emotional effects of this ceremonial on their worshippers as of primary importance. Nonetheless, such effects may occur and they may be of importance to the worshippers. The dignified ritual, the smell of incense, the ceremonial vestments, and the numerous candles in a Roman or Eastern Mass may all create or intensify feelings of awe amongst the worshippers. Such postures as standing or kneeling in prayer may not only symbolise the attitudes of reverence and submission; they may also create the emotions appropriate to these attitudes.

The use of music is also a means of inducing emotional experience in worshippers. This function is most obvious when the music is not a prescribed part of the service but is improvised at points where intensification of feeling is the aim, as in the soft music which may be, played while an evangelical preacher is reiterating his appeal for converts to come up to the mercy seat. In some religious bodies, short hymns of highly emotional character are repeated with semi-hypnotic effect and are strongly evocative of emotional responses.

The great inducer of emotion is, however, human language, particularly in those religious bodies which have abandoned the induction of emotion by visual ceremonial. One psychological characteristic of the religious reformation of the sixteenth century could indeed be described as an abandonment of vision and gesture as means to religious experience and the substitution of the spoken word.

Obviously not all words spoken in preaching have the purpose of inducing emotion. A religious address may have the object of imparting information or of directing the hearers to some desirable course of action. It may, however, have as its object the arousal of some kind of emotion, either for its own sake, in which case the emotional response of the audience is a measure of how far the address has achieved its aim, or as an adjunct to religious revivals, where it is a means of inducing the crisis of religious conversion. This emotional oratory was probably commoner in the last half of the nineteenth century than it is at the present day.

We are here, no doubt, in a region in which individual differences are important. Some individuals may find themselves little affected emotionally by the visual perception of ceremonial and regard it as meaningless fuss. Others are little affected emotionally by the auditory experience of hearing music, and feel it is an unprofitable part of the religious rite. Others are relatively indifferent to the effects of emotional oratory; they may prefer that the preacher should confine himself to factual communication or exhortation to desirable behaviour. Such differences and their relation to preferred forms of worship do not seem to have been made the subject of any systematic psychological study. They would seem to be a promising subject of future research study with obvious practical implications for the question of how far uniformity of religious practice is an attainable or desirable end.

There should also be considered the possibility of a more general individual difference covering the degree to which emotional experience, however induced, is required or tolerated in religious services. Some religious services of the Pentecostalist type aim at inducing a considerable level of emotional experience in the worshippers, and those accustomed to such services may find more conventional worship dull and unsatisfying. If the full range of psychological requirements are to be satisfied in religious worship, it may be that a considerable range of rite will be required, differing not only in the visual or auditory elements that may be used in the induction of emotional religious experiences, but also in the extent to which there is any attempt to induce emotional experience; both highly emotional and emotionally neutral forms of worship may serve the needs of different worshippers.

It has been suggested earlier that there is a distinction between the forms of worship in which the induction of emotion is valued as a means to attain some end, such as conversion, and the worship of those religious bodies for which the arousing of an emotional response is itself regarded as having a religious value. This value may be expressed as the visible sign of the working of the Holy Spirit. Religious services of the latter kind are found more commonly in the United States than in Great Britain. I have, in an American 'Church of God', seen a preacher with perspiration pouring down his face while he vigorously poured out a stream of emotive language. The distinctive feature of this kind of service is that it is not directed towards producing any permanent change in the members of the congregation but rather at inducing in them an emotional experience, which experience is regarded as good in itself. This does not, of course, imply that the experience may not also bear fruit in the lives of the worshippers; any body which practised the induction of emotion in its meetings for worship would claim that it did.

The induction of emotion in religious services may also be accompanied by various behaviour phenomena such as semi-automatic dancing. One of the most curious of these emotion inducing congregations that I have had the opportunity of observing was in Durham, North Carolina, in which the handling of poisonous snakes was the central part of the service. They were usually rattle-snakes, but copper-heads were also reported to have been used. There was the usual working up of an emotional state in the congregation by passionate oratory and the congregation started handling snakes when they were already in a semi-ecstatic condition. The handling of the snakes was partly a test of their condition; partly also it may have helped to induce the condition through the tension of fear. Fatal accidents did sometimes take place but they seem to have been very rare. A police raid confirmed the important fact that the poison fangs of the snakes had not been removed. A state law prohibiting the handling of rattle-snakes in public brought this type of service to an end in the town, although it is still said to go on in camp-meetings in the forest. When I last attended the service it still had the essential pattern of induction of emotion by oratory but it seemed then to have become relatively ineffective. Something vital to the induction of emotion seemed to have gone out with the disappearance of the snakes.

A more restrained form of worship with induction of emotion as a central feature is to be found in the Pentecostal churches of which the 'Assemblies of God' can be taken as typical. These developed out of the holiness movement within Methodism which started as a reaction against liberal protestantism during the last half of the nineteenth century. This movement asserted the literal inspiration of the Bible, the need for personal experience of salvation and for moral perfection in the individual.[5] The services of the Pentecostal churches include emotional oratory and the repetitive singing of short hymns with a strong feeling element. One of their characteristic features is the occurrence of semi-automatic unintelligible speech, *glossolalia* or speaking with tongues.

Glossolalia has a long history in the Christian Church. Its occurrence is reported at the first Pentecost after the crucifixion (Acts, 2.4). It is also commented on by St Paul as one of the standard elements in the early Christian religious services (1 Corinthians, 14.5, and elsewhere in the same epistle).*

It seems also to have happened sporadically throughout the history of the Christian churches, sometimes welcomed as a gift of the Spirit, sometimes accepted with reluctance as a strange abnormality. One of the early modern appearances of speaking with tongues was amongst the congregation of the well-known and popular preacher Edward Irving who was minister of a Caledonian chapel in Regent's Square, London, in the first half of the nineteenth century. It had a somewhat mixed reception. Irving himself, after some initial hesitation, welcomed it as the answer to his prayer for the renewal of spiritual gifts, and spoke of a new 'order of prophets ... who, being filled with the Holy Ghost, do speak with tongues and prophesy'.[6] Others were less impressed. Irving's friend, Thomas Carlyle, referred to these events as 'the most doleful of all phenomena'.[7] When he was charged with allowing unauthorised persons to speak in his church, the London Presbytery decided that Irving had rendered himself unfit to remain their minister. Irving himself and the modern Pentecostalists consider that speaking with tongues has high spiritual value. A typical testimony is one quoted by Kelsey: 'As I knelt to pray ... to my amazement I heard myself speaking words unfamiliar to me. It lifted me into a higher realm and gave me a sense of the nearness of God.'[5] This, of course, is the important aspect of glossolalia, but it is not one on which psychology can have much to say. From the psychological point of view, glossolalia is a speech automatism arising under certain conditions of expectancy, which is commonly felt by those experiencing it to be a valuable ingredient in their religious lives. It is not a phenomenon peculiar to Christianity; it has been shown to be widespread and ancient in non-Christian religions of certain types, particularly those which have a tradition of spirit possession and in which inspired speech is a recognised cultural element.[8]

There is some difference of opinion as to whether the utterances of glossolalia are sounds belonging to no intelligible speech or whether they belong to some speech not understood by the auditors. There is also some difference of opinion as to whether the sounds are repetitive elements of simple structure, as asserted by Cutten[9] or a language flow of complex structure, as reported by Kelsey.[5] Such questions should now be settled by analysis of tape-recorded specimens of glossolalia. It seems not unlikely that both forms would be found.

* The passage here referred to is: 'Now I want you all to speak in tongues, but even more to prophesy' (RSV). 'Speak in tongues' is a literal translation of the Greek original and conveys the meaning well enough. The *New English Bible* has 'ecstatic utterance' instead of 'speaking with tongues'. This is objectionable as obscuring the psychological distinction between glossolalia and prophecy. It appears that Paul used both terms to refer to a form of ecstatic utterance and that the difference between them was that prophecy was in intelligible speech while glossolalia was not.

THE EMOTIONAL FACTOR    55

In addition to the emission of speech sounds which form no recognisable part of any known language, there is also to be found the semi-automatic utterance of meaningful speech. This also was found in the congregation of Edward Irving and, after a time, became more important to the congregation than the speaking with tongues. Irving identified these utterances with the 'prophecy' referred to by St Paul, and accepted instructions received in this way as authoritative for the guidance of his congregation. In religious bodies where such utterances are accepted, they are commonly attributed to the activity of the Holy Spirit. The prophetic utterances in Irving's congregation that have been recorded for us do not seem to justify this claim for them. They seem to be commonplace and repetitive, reinforced by meaningless interjections. For example, Irving said in the course of one of his sermons: 'Shut not the Lord out, the Spirit of the Lord speaking in His servants.' A voice then broke out: 'Oh! I have set before thee an open door; Oh! Let no man shut it; Oh! let no man shut it'.[6] This adds nothing material to what the preacher had said, and seems to have no quality that would suggest an intrusion from the spiritual world. Another prophetic interruption of the same discourse was: 'Ah! will ye despise – ah! will ye despise the blood of Jesus? Will ye pass by the Cross, the Cross of Jesus? Oh! Oh! Oh! will ye crucify the Lord of Glory?' This too seems to contain nothing to suggest a more exalted source than a human memory abundantly stored with scriptural phrases. Irving himself seems to have supposed that all such semi-automatic utterances were either divinely inspired or results of the activity of 'lying spirits'. He was content to validate them by a very simple test of orthodoxy in response, in order to rule out the possibility of their being products of lying spirits. There is, however, also the possibility of their being the product of the subconscious mental activity of the person producing them, or, if it is agreed that spiritual inspiration may be at work in them, of this inspiration being diluted by sub-conscious activity. There are, therefore, good psychological grounds for refusing to treat such semi-automatic utterances as authoritative either as guides to belief or as directives of behaviour. It is not surprising to find that the later history of Irvingism is one of increasing control of 'prophetic utterances' by authority.[10]

We do not know what kind of semi-automatic utterance in the early Corinthian congregations was referred to by St Paul as 'prophesying'. That it was confined to some members of the congregation is shown by the reference to it as one of many possible gifts possessed by different individuals (1 Cor. 12.10). It was an activity of which St Paul thought highly; 'he who prophesies speaks to men for their upbuilding and encouragement and consolation ... Now I want you all to speak in tongues, but even more to prophesy' (1 Cor. 14.3 and 5). St Paul's approval of this practice suggests that its customary utterances were of a higher order than the recorded interruptions of the 'prophets' of Irving's congregation. His reference to 'upbuilding and encouragement and consolation' seems also to imply that fore-telling of the future was not more than a minor part of the prophet's activity. It seems likely that what he meant by 'prophesying' was an activity more resembling the moving and eloquent sermons of Irving himself than the banalities of his interruptors. These sermons were earnest and sincere, although their moving quality was due to their departure from the standards of rational discourse. They were based on emotional rather than rational use of language.

Wherever there is promotion of the affective side of religion, whether by chewing of peyote, listening to sacred music, or being stirred by emotional oratory, the question may be asked whether such arousing of religious emotion is an end in itself or whether its usefulness lies in lasting effects on the behaviour and the devotional life of the persons experiencing it. While the psychologist may not feel concerned to make a judgment as to the religious value of feeling states which do not lead to consequences in behaviour, he may usefully point out some psychological considerations which bear on this problem.

An emotional state (such as fear, anger, or joy) is a condition of the organism which has mental and bodily aspects. On the mental side there is a distinctive feeling-tone or affect which may be pleasurable or unpleasurable. On the bodily side there are certain physiological events connected with the activity of the primitive autonomic nervous system. Such changes are: flushing, turning pale, increased rapidity of heart beat, changes in breathing rate, etc. These may all be regarded as parts of the preparation of the body for some activity, such as making an attack or flying from danger. Emotion can, in fact, be regarded on its physiological side as a mobilisation of the organism for the carrying out of some more or less strenuous course of behaviour.

For the human organism, the activity towards which an emotion is directed may be of a less primitive type than such simple responses as aggression or flight. The emotion of pity may lead to the behaviour of relieving distress, reverence may lead to self-abasement, and anger may lead to fighting against injustice rather than to aggression against an individual. It still remains true, however, that the biological function of emotion is to initiate action. There is a possibility that the induction of emotion by emotional oratory or otherwise in a religious service may lead to the induced emotional state being regarded as an end in itself and ceasing to be a stimulus to action. Such divorce of emotion from its outcome in action has been called *sentimentalism*. This meaning of the word has been illustrated by a story of a Russian lady weeping over the troubles of fictitious people on the stage while her coachman was freezing to death on the pavement outside. Sentimentalism is a possible outcome of a strongly emotional religion if its emotions are enjoyed for their own sake and cease to be spurs to action. It is generally held by religious persons that the important result of religious feeling is stimulation to devotion and good behaviour with respect to one's fellow-men, and that it is by its success in contributing to these ends that the value of religious emotion must be judged.

## REFERENCES

1. W. James, *The varieties of religious experience*, London, 1903.
2. A. Huxley, *The doors of perception*, London, 1954.
3. J. S. Slotkin, 'Menomini peyotism', *Transactions of the American Philosophical Society* N. S., XLII, Philadelphia, 1952, pp. 565–700.
4. W. H. Pahnke. 'Drugs and mysticism', *International Journal of Parapsychology*, VIII, 1966, pp. 295–320.
5. M. T. Kelsey. *Speaking with tongues: an experiment in spiritual experience*, London, 1965.
6. Margaret Oliphant, *The life of Edward Irving*, vol. II, London, 1862.
7. Thomas Carlyle, *Reminiscences*, vol. I, (Ed. J. A. Froude). London, 1881.
8. L. C. May, 'A survey of glossolalia and related phenomena in non-Christian religions', *American Anthropologist*, LVIII, Menaska (Wis.), 1956, pp. 75–96.
9. G. B. Cutten. *Speaking with tongues: historically and psychologically considered*, New Haven, 1927.
10. E. Miller, *The history and doctrine of Irvingism*, London, 1878, (2 vols.).

# 8. Religion and human needs

Those who have speculated about the origins of religion have often put forward the idea that it is a response to needs not fully satisfied in this world. The basic need of primitive man is security against such threats as famine, disease, and destruction by his enemies. Much of his everyday life in hunting, agriculture, etc. is directed towards avoiding these dangers, although he does not altogether succeed in removing them. To these safeguarding activities, he adds other means for security derived from his belief in a spiritual world: ritual actions and petitionary prayers, which are also regarded as protecting him. This hope of obtaining security by the utilisation of spiritual forces may be surmised to be one of the roots of the religious attitude. The threats to a member of a modern civilised community are not identical: the fear of famine is remote, but that of disease remains present, while that of destruction by war is greater than ever before. The religious man may still pray, as in the Litany of the Church of England, for deliverance: 'from plague, pestilence, and famine; from battle and murder and from sudden death'. Modern man is still insecure in face of the dangers that threaten him; he may still employ petitionary prayer as one of the means of protection against these insecurities.

Security against hostile environmental forces is likely, however, to be a less strong driving force towards the development of a religious attitude than is the need for security in social relationships. Every human being needs the security and consistency of motivation given by the sense of loving and of being loved. If his ordinary life does not satisfy these needs, he may be driven to find other satisfaction in drugs or he may develop the hatred for other people which leads to crime. The deprivation of love may lead the deprived person to the psychiatrist's consulting room. Alternatively he may find in religious life the satisfaction which his ordinary social life denies him. When the Reverend David Wilkerson started work amongst the gangs of New York, he found they were adolescents full of bitterness and hatred who took drugs and engaged in gang warfare.[1] The beginning of the religious message that he took to them was that God loved them. When they accepted this, the process of conversion to the religious attitude began, and led to the disappearance of the previous attitudes of hatred and often to a cessation of the craving for drugs. The needs to love and to be loved arise as the emotional component of the sex instinct. Their part in the religious life may be expressed by saying that the needs of the sex-instinct, like those of the instinct of self-preservation, may be a part of the foundation of the religious attitude.

There are a number of different lines of evidence that suggest a connection between the sex instinct and the religious attitude. There is first the fact of correlation between some developmental phases of sexuality and of religion. One of the most striking of these is the strong development of religious interest that takes place at the time of adolescence, in particular the phenomenon of adolescent religious conversion which will be discussed in Chapter 14. Starbuck was the first to collect statistical evidence in support of the commonly held opinion that conversion is primarily an adolescent phenomenon.[2] His finding was that conversions 'begin to occur at seven or eight years and increase in number gradually, to ten or eleven, and then rapidly to sixteen; rapidly decline to twenty, and gradually fall away after that'. His conclusion was that: 'Conversion and puberty tend to supplement each other in time rather than to coincide; but they may, nevertheless, be mutually conditioned.'

While the tendency of religious conversion to occur at the time of adolescence may be considered as an indication that this religious crisis may be partly conditioned by the development of the sex instinct at that time, the correlation is not close at other periods of life. In particular, as William James pointed out, 'the religious age *par excellence* would seem to be old age, when the uproar of the sexual life is past'.[3] The opinion that old age is the period of maximum development of the religious attitude is confirmed by more recent empirical studies of the relation between age and a positive attitude towards religion. Argyle quotes a number of quantitative investigations of this problem, including one by Cavan who studied a sample of 1,200 people with ages ranging from 60 to 100.[4] It showed a clear tendency for acceptance of a religious position to rise through this range of ages, while acceptance of the reality of an after-life rose to 100 per cent after the age of 90. This increase of religious involvement after the age of sexual activity has passed has been used as an argument against the view that sexual frustration is the sole factor in the production of the religious attitude. There is, however, some exaggeration in the statement that, in old age, the sexual life is past. While the urge to mating behaviour may have disappeared the more general need to love and be loved has by no means disappeared in old age. Indeed, it may be less satisfied then, and so add its quota to other psychological factors that in old age become more effective in contributing to the religious attitude.

Further evidence of the same kind is provided by investigating how far religious conviction is correlated with degree of sexual frustration. No enquiry seems to give a direct answer to this question; 'degree of sexual frustration' is a factor not easy to reduce to quantitative terms. A rough indication is, however, given by the finding of Gorer that the religious activity of the single is somewhat greater than that of the married, while that of the widowed is considerably greater than either.[4] This finding is consistent with the hypothesis that religious activity is inversely correlated with the degree of satisfaction of the sex instinct which is what would be expected if sexual deprivation were one factor in the drive behind religious behaviour.

A striking piece of evidence in this connection is the tendency of religious emotion to be expressed in the language of human love. This is often found among mystical writers. St John of the Cross, for example, describes the mystical union in the following stanzas:

> On my flowery bosom, kept whole for Him alone, there He reposed and slept; and I cherished Him, and the waving of the cedars fanned Him.
>
> As his hair floated in the breeze, that from the turret blew, He struck me on the neck, with His gentle hand. and all sensation left me.
>
> I continued in oblivion lost. my head was resting on my love; lost to all things and myself, and, amid the lilies forgotten, threw all my cares away.[5]

This would seem to be in origin the language of human love, which is found not only in the writings of the mystics but also in such popular devotions as hymns. The best known example is, perhaps, Charles Wesley's well known hymn beginning 'Love Divine, all loves excelling'. The use of the language of human love as a symbol for religious love is found also in the acceptance of such a work as the *Song of Solomon* as expressing the love of Christ for his Church, and in the Hindu religion of the loves of Krishna and the milkmaids as symbols of divine love.[6]

All the same, this use of the language of human love is not such as would support a theory which asserts the identity of human love and religious feeling. Mystics and other devotional writers are faced by the inadequacy of the literal use of language to provide descriptions of the experiences they are concerned with. To overcome this inadequacy they adopt a use of symbolism which is drawn from various aspects of life. They speak of a divine lover, of betrothals and of spiritual marriage, but they also use the symbolism of light and darkness, of listening to music, and of tasting and smelling.

Another indication of the importance of this factor in religious development is the high value placed by religious bodies on chastity, partial or complete. Chastity is the suppression of the behaviour of the sex instinct. It may be partial in the case of the ordinary religious individual who is permitted sexual activity provided that it is canalised within the limits of monogamy. But for those undergoing further spiritual development more is required. Absolute chastity, the complete denial of the consolations of human love, is generally regarded as an essential condition for the religious contemplative's enjoyment of divine love. Equally it was regarded by the Buddha as an essential condition for the attainment of the complete emancipation of the Arahat.

On the other hand, it must be noticed that, in their suppression as a condition for the more advanced religious developments, the sex impulses do not stand alone. In the ascetic practices that lead to the contemplative life, meekness, fasting and solitude are highly valued as well as chastity. Meekness is the characteristic of behaviour that accompanies the suppression of the self-assertive impulses, fasting is the behaviour of suppressing the impulses of nutritional craving, solitude is the suppression of the very strong gregarious behaviour tendencies. The purpose of this ascetic training is obviously that of the overcoming of all craving and not only the craving that belongs to sex.

Sexuality has been a favourite choice of those who derive religious behaviour from a single psychological root. The evidence would seem rather to suggest that it is one of many roots. Even the idea that it is one of many roots has been regarded as so discreditable to religion that the mere enumeration of points of connection between religion and sexuality was at one time supposed to be a fatal criticism of religion. Such criticism has little force at the present day. The work of Freud and the psychoanalysts has accustomed us to the possibility that the sex instinct may provide driving forces behind a number of human activities, some good and some bad, and to the idea that this is as respectable an origin for human drives as any other of our instinctive impulses. We are ready now to accept William James's dictum that it is by their fruits and not by their roots that the value of human activities must be judged.

The religious man may indeed recognise the connection between human sexual love and religious love, and regard the love of God as the final purpose for which human love exists. Thus Coventry Patmore has written of 'that human love which is the precursor and explanation of and initiation into the divine'.[7] The same thought, of human love as a means to divine love, is expressed by the Muslim poet Jami:

> Even from earthly love thy face avert not,
> Since to the Real it may serve to raise thee.
> Ere A, B, C are rightly apprehended,
> How canst thou con the pages of the Kur'an?

> For, should'st thou fear to drink wine from Form's flagon,
> Thou canst not drain the draught of the ideal.

But yet beware! Be not by Form belated;
Strive rather with all speed the bridge to traverse.
If to the bourn thou fain would'st bear thy baggage
Upon the bridge let not thy footsteps linger.[8]

If a lack of love is one of the marks of the individual to whom religion has much to offer, so also is the absence of a normal amount of self-esteem. Those who are driven to drugs and delinquency by lovelessness often show in addition a degree of dissatisfaction with themselves which amounts to self-hatred. It would be a considerable misunderstanding of the matter to suppose that the religious attitude offers alternative grounds for self-esteem based on spiritual factors. All religions condemn such an attitude as spiritual pride which is regarded as an impediment to the religious way of life. It is rather an abandonment of self-esteem in complete 'self-naughting' that is regarded as the proper component of the religious attitude. In Buddhism this rejection of the self is carried so far that an essential part of its conceptual system is the denial of the reality of the self. The consistent Buddhist cannot love himself because he has learned to believe that he has no 'self' to love; his love can then be given to other living beings. Although this reason for it is peculiar to Buddhism, the requirement of abandonment of self-esteem is an element of all religions. How then can a religious attitude demanding the abandonment of self-esteem have anything to offer those whose behaviour problems largely result from self-hatred? I suggest that the answer is that the achievement of self-naughting in the religious sense is destructive of both self-esteem and self-hatred. If one regards oneself simply as an instrument for the carrying out of the divine will, self-esteem and self-hatred are equally irrelevant and the energy behind these sentiments may be liberated for love of others.

Another human need contributing to the religious attitude is the necessity that every man has of adjusting himself to the fact that his life will come to an end sooner or later. The fact of death is, of course universal amongst living organisms; it is reasonable to suppose that man alone can formulate this expectation in words and finds it desirable to adopt an attitude to it which renders it tolerable. The obvious way of achieving this end in our own culture is to accept the belief that human life continues beyond the grave. This may be the case; there is insufficient ground for condemning this expectation as illusory merely because it coincides with human hopes. Although the point of view of modern biological science is opposed to the expectation of survival after death, there is some empirical evidence (to be discussed in Chapter 11) that such survival is a reality. Belief in survival is not, however, a necessary part of the religious adjustment to the fact of death; it is generally stated not to have been adopted by early Judaism. Nor is the expectation of survival always regarded as a means of reduction of anxiety about death. In the early Buddhist Scriptures, continued existence is regarded rather as a nightmare from which one must be delivered by following the teachings of the Buddha. Thus the Buddha said, in one of his last addresses:

> It is through not understanding and grasping four Noble Truths, O brethren, that we have had to run so long, to wander so long in this weary path of transmigration, both you and I! ... But when these noble truths are grasped and known the craving for existence is rooted out, that which leads to renewed existence is destroyed, and then there is no more birth![9]

Even when belief in a future life was strong during the Middle Ages, it was by no means consolatory; the general opinion was that one's most likely destination for the future life was hell which was thought of as an eternal concentration camp to which extinction at death would be decidedly preferable. At the present time, in our own culture, the idea of a future life is more generally held in a consolatory form. It would still be superficial to regard it as necessarily illusory. Whether conscious existence goes on after death is a question of fact which may, in principle, be decided by empirical methods, although human wishes may influence one's expectations about the character of life after death.

The offering of the possibility of a belief in continued existence after death is not the only contribution that a religious attitude can make towards the acceptance of death. Perhaps more fundamental is the point that the religious view, of a spiritual world within which earthly life is a mere episode, reduces the importance of the termination of that episode. Death is then regarded not as the end of everything but as an incident in an eternal drama and the prospect of death becomes tolerable.

The idea that the adjustment to death is one of the essential factors in the religious attitude is one that forces itself on any reader of religious literature. The mode of adjustment may be different: belief in a consolatory image of the after-life amongst modern Christians, reflection on the transitoriness of all compounded things amongst the Buddhists. Perhaps the most important empirical evidence for the relationship between the religious attitude and adjustment to the fact of death is that already mentioned: the increased tendency to religious acceptance amongst the old, and, in particular, their high degree of acceptance of the doctrine of immortality. Argyle has pointed to the latter fact as evidence that belief in immortality is a product of the fear of death.[4] For this to be a valid conclusion would, however, require that we knew that the fear of death increased with old age. Of this increase there is no evidence and common experience would lead one to suppose rather that the fear of death declines with old age.

What undoubtedly does increase in old age is the immediacy of the problem of death and the mental necessity to come to terms with it.

This may not, however, be the only factor favouring belief in immortality in old age. There may also be an increasing tendency for the idea of the self to become detached from that of the physical body. In such states of affliction as harsh imprisonment and disabling disease it is found that an attitude develops of regarding the body as an object, and feeling oneself to be an observer looking on at the affliction of the body.[10] This attitude, called by some psychiatrists by the disparaging name of *depersonalisation*, may well be increased with increasing infirmity of the body in old age. It is obviously an attitude favourable to the development of a belief in immortality, and also favourable to the adoption of a religious attitude towards life and death. This tendency to loss of self-identification with the body may, therefore, as well as the increased immediacy of death, be a factor in determining the religious attitudes of old age.

## REFERENCES

1.  D. Wilkerson, *The cross and the switchblade*, London, 1963.
2.  E. D. Starbuck, *The psychology of religion*, London, 1899.
3.  W. James, *The varieties of religious experience*, London, 1902.
4.  M. Argyle, *Religious behaviour*, London, 1958.
5.  St John of the Cross, *The dark night of the soul* (English trans.), London, 1916.
6.  W. G. Archer, *The loves of Krishna*, London, 1957.
7.  Coventry Patmore, *The rod, the root and the flower*, London, 1895.
8.  E. G. Browne, *A year amongst the Persians*, London, 1893.
9.  T. W. Rhys Davids, (Trans.), 'Maha-Parinibbana-Sutta', *Sacred Books of the East*, xi, Oxford, 1881.
10. Elie A. Cohen, *Human behaviour in the concentration camp* (Engl. trans.), London, 1954.

# 9. The intellectual factor in religion

No one would now hold the view that religion is primarily a product of intellectual processes. Such factors as the influence of one's social environment and the activity of vague unverbalised feelings are generally recognised as parts of the foundation of the religious attitude which are likely to precede any kind of rational thinking about it. Yet the ability to think in words and to use words as a means of discriminating between the true and the false is an important human achievement which may be expected to have its influence on the development of the religious attitude. Amongst some writers on religion, the reaction against regarding it as a product of intellectual thought has gone so far that religion is treated as wholly a product of irrational factors and the reasons given in its support are regarded as mere rationalisations which have no influence on the system of belief.

This term 'rationalisation' was introduced by Trotter to stand for a verbal process used to provide justification for a belief held on other grounds.[1] An extreme form of it is found in certain kinds of insanity, as in *paranoia* or *delusional insanity* in which the patient's belief in his own grandeur or in the persecutions he suffers from other people are supported by processes of reasoning which may be systematic and coherent, but which are essentially irrational in the sense that they are not based on correct appreciation of the situation but on needs and cravings of the patient. Not much less irrational may be the sane person's 'reasons' for believing in the wickedness of the enemy and the virtue of his own side during a war. The term may also be usefully extended to the somewhat irrational verbal reactions of normal people whose minds supply them with reasons for opinions based on emotional grounds, as when they produce reasoned arguments for the iniquity of a tax which they resent because it presses hardly on themselves. In this sense of the word, it can hardly be doubted that rationalisation plays a part in the building up of a religious belief system as it does in any other system of beliefs into which emotional elements also enter. The concept of rationalisation is indeed a necessary tool for the understanding of such a belief system. It does not, however, provide a means of deciding whether a particular system of beliefs is true or false, or whether the arguments used in defence of it are sound or unsound. All that is implied by calling an argument a 'rationalisation' is that there are other, perhaps stronger reasons for holding the belief in question than those contained in the argument used in its defence. The concept of rationalisation is often used in controversy as a too easy means of condemning beliefs without enquiry into the problem of whether or not they are true.

Acceptance of the process of rationalisation does not, however, give ground for the opinion that a man's intellectual processes have no influence on his beliefs. Their influence may be less than is commonly supposed but it remains true that a belief is more confidently held if a process of thought can be made to justify it, and most people tend to abandon beliefs which seem to them to have inadequate intellectual support even when these beliefs are attractive to them on other grounds. In fact, the tendency to produce rationalisations is itself an indication of the instability of a belief lacking supporting intellectual grounds. The extent to which such grounds must be logically valid before they are accepted as supports is a matter in which individuals differ very much. At one extreme is the paranoiac whose intellectual processes are entirely subservient to his psychological needs and impervious to contrary evidence. At the other extreme would be the entirely rational individual whose opinions were determined only by rational processes and not at all by his needs or wishes. The normal individual lies somewhere between these extremes, having his opinions partly determined by his hopes and fears, partly by the adequacy of the rational grounds he can find for holding them.

If it is agreed that intellectual processes form part of the foundation for a religious attitude, it does not follow that this intellectual foundation is expressed by the traditional arguments for the existence of God. The 'ontological argument', for instance states that, since God is defined as a perfect being, and since existence is necessarily a part of perfection, it follows that God exists. This argument has seemed coercive to some philosophers in the past; in somewhat varying forms it was maintained by St Anselm, by Descartes, and by Leibnitz. Later philosophers have generally followed Kant in condemning it as faulty in logic, but even if the argument were logically adequate, it would remain psychologically inadequate as a means of creating religious conviction. One could not convince an unbeliever of God's existence by putting to him the ontological argument; it would seem to him merely a verbal trick. Nor is it of psychological value as a means of strengthening the faith of the average religious believer; indeed, he might find his religious faith somewhat shaken if he could be convinced that it rested on such dubious grounds as this.

If the ontological argument for the existence of God is not itself a psychological cause of belief, it may nevertheless be an expression in verbal form of something more vague which is a genuine cause of belief. Many religious people feel convinced of the reality of God even though they may not feel that they can give any adequate intellectual ground for this belief. They may indeed find themselves so strongly convinced of its truth that they are unable to believe the opposite statement that there is no God. The ontological argument can perhaps be regarded as a verbalised expression of this conviction. In other words, the ontological argument may be considered to be a rationalisation of the intuitive conviction that God must exist.

The other arguments for the existence of God may be regarded in the same way. There is, for example, the argument from design: that, in the structure of living things and in their inter-relations, there seems to be evidence of design similar to that which we find in a humanly devised mechanical system such as a watch, and that the presence of design implies a designer. This argument was at one time widely accepted but it has been progressively eroded by the progress of science. The theory of organic evolution suggested that the appearance of design might be due to a blind process of natural selection of those plants or animals whose variations happened to be favourable to survival. It has been further weakened in more recent times by the discovery that some of the processes that give an impression of design, such as those of growth, may be explained as resulting from the properties of complex organic molecules. Yet, if it is weak as an intellectual ground for religious belief, the argument from design may be a true indication of a way of feeling. It may be regarded as a rationalisation of the vague but strong feeling that the way things are shows the handiwork of a personal designer and this may be one of the psychological grounds for religious belief. Other people, of course, may be convinced that the world shows lack of purpose and design and this may be a psychological ground for religious unbelief.

An example of the early stages of the reflective thought that accompanies the growth of the religious attitude is quoted by Ribot. The speaker was a Basuto herdsman:

Twelve years ago, I went to feed my flocks. The weather was hazy. I sat down upon a rock and asked myself sorrowful questions; yes, sorrowful, because I was unable to answer them. Who has touched the stars with his hands? On what pillars do they rest? I asked myself. The waters are never weary; they know no other law than to flow without ceasing – from morning till night, and from night till morning; but where do they stop? And who makes them flow thus? The clouds also come and go, and burst in water over the earth. Whence come they? Who sends them? The diviners certainly do not give us rain; for how could they do it? And why do I not see them with my own eyes, when they go up to heaven to fetch it? ... I cannot see the wind; but what is it? Who brings it, makes it blow? ... Then I buried my face in both my hands.[2]

The actual questions asked are, of course, determined by the cultural situation of the individual asking; many of them would seem to us now to be the kind of questions that must be solved by scientific investigation and not by the activity of thinking. Other cultures ask other questions. An uneducated Indian herdsman might, for example, be more likely to ask the questions which were asked by Gautama Buddha at the beginning of his quest: 'What is sorrow? What are the causes of sorrow? and, What is the way to end sorrow?' Another system of religious questions was asked of Paulinus, the Christian missionary to the Saxons, by one of the chief men of King Edwin of Northumbria:

> The present life of man, O King, seems to me ... like to the swift flight of a sparrow through the room wherein you sit at supper in winter ... So this life of man appears for a short space, but of what went before, or what is to follow, we are utterly ignorant. If, therefore, this new doctrine contains something more certain, it seems justly to deserve to be followed.[3]

Different religious systems have given different answers to such questions, and religious systems growing up under different cultural situations have found that different questions are asked. It seems, however, always to be the case that one of the functions of a religious system of thought is to satisfy human curiosity on questions that are not easily answered and that may be remote from everyday practical concerns. These answers, when accepted, serve the psychological function of allaying anxiety by reducing uncertainty and of providing a guide to behaviour. It is true that the religious leader may refuse to answer some questions on the ground that the answers would not serve any useful religious end. Thus it is reported that when one of his monks approached the Buddha to ask whether the world was eternal and infinite, whether the soul and body were or were not identical, and whether the liberated one exists or does not exist after death, the Buddha's reply was that the religious life did not depend on the answers to these questions, so his teaching did not answer them. On the other hand, he had explained the origin of sorrow, the cessation of sorrow, and the path leading to the cessation of sorrow, because these things were concerned with the fundamentals of religion, and led to the religious ends of passionlessness and wisdom.[4]

The questions that different religious systems claim to answer are somewhat different; the answers which they regard as acceptable are often very different, even between different branches of a single religion. The answers given in a particular religious system are what we commonly call its system of dogma. From a psychological point of view, a dogmatic system may be regarded as a set of factual or quasi-factual statements to which assent is required or expected from members of a particular religious group. What is meant by calling them 'quasi-factual' is that they are in the form of statements as to what is the case although they may not be verifiable in any of the ways in which we should normally expect to be able to verify a factual statement.

There are obvious differences in the amount of dogma in different religious traditions and in the extent to which different religious bodies tolerate deviations from the standard (or orthodox) responses to dogmatic statements. These differences are sometimes exaggerated: it is said, for example, that Buddhism differs from Christianity in having no system of dogmas. If, however, one reads the Buddhist Scriptures one finds many statements of a factual or quasi-factual order to which the Buddhist is expected to assent. The Buddhist belief that one is re-incarnated after death is a dogma no less than the Christian doctrine of the resurrection of the body. The holding of 'right views' was moreover one element in the noble eightfold way taught by the Buddha as the road to enlightenment. Nonetheless, there is clearly a quantitative difference between Christianity and Buddhism both with respect to the number of dogmatic statements the member is expected to accept and in the extent of the social disapproval of deviations from this expected assent. If one imagines a diagram with axes representing amount of dogma and degree of intolerance of individual deviations from dogmatic standards, then most Christian bodies would have to be represented by points further along these axes than would Buddhist groups.

Even within Christianity, different bodies would be represented at different distances along these axes; so also would the same religious body at different periods of its history. If we confine ourselves to the more easily observable of these two factors, the degree of intolerance of dogmatic deviations, we can judge of its strength in different bodies and at different times by using the criterion of the violence of behaviour directed against the deviating individual. This attained its maximum in the days of religious persecution when deviations from orthodoxy were punished by death by burning. This was for many centuries an accepted mode of behaviour in many Christian bodies, Catholic and Protestant. A few only did not show the over-valuation of acceptance of orthodoxy which is implied by persecution, notably the Society of Friends and the Unitarians. The persecution of heretics is a social phenomenon which requires psychological understanding not merely as a historical curiosity but also as a symptom of an attitude which has by no means disappeared at the present day. A rational explanation would be that it was a vain attempt to secure uniformity of belief, but it is probable that it was also the result of strong affective pressures and of an irrational desire for security against the threat of the innovator.

There are a number of questions about the intellectual foundation of the religious attitude which invite empirical methods of study: some have been investigated although much more remains to be found out about all of them. There are, for example, certain questions that may be asked about the strength with which the beliefs of a religious dogmatic system are held and of how this strength varies between different individuals. These questions are not of merely academic importance since the answers to them have obvious bearings on the practical problems of religious intolerance.

Some years ago, I made an investigation of this problem with a group of people of varying age and social backgrounds.[5] Each of the experimental subjects was given a typed sheet of statements, some of a religious order (e.g. 'There is a personal God') and some of a non-religious kind (as 'Green is a primary colour'). For each statement, they were asked to indicate the degree of conviction with which it was accepted or rejected by them, using a seven-point scale ranging from +3 for certainty that the statement was true, to −3 for complete certainty that it was false, lesser degrees of conviction being indicated by +2 and +1 and no conviction whatever by 0. For each individual, or for the group as a whole, one could then calculate an 'index of certainty' as the average numerical value of the degrees of conviction recorded.

The general finding was that, although there was division of opinion as to whether statements were true or false, there was a general tendency for the degree of conviction to be high; the experimental subjects tended to be certain or nearly certain that an assertion was true or that it was false, while a lower degree of conviction was relatively rare. This tendency to certainty was not absent from non-religious statements but was less in amount for these; the average index of certainty for the religious statements was found to be 2.13 while that for the non-religious statements was only 1.58. These figures are, of course, derived only from a single sample and cannot be taken to be generally applicable. It is, however, encouraging to find that Professor Brown, carrying out a parallel experiment on a group in Adelaide (South Australia) obtained very similar figures. He found, for example, an average index of certainty of 2.1 for religious statements and 1.56 for non-religious ones. This is surprisingly close to those I had found in Glasgow many years before.[6]

I was also interested in the question of what sort of people showed high certainty and whether this was peculiar to believers. For the second question I needed also an index of orthodoxy which was calculated for each individual by taking the mean degree of certainty he showed for each statement but counting as negative any certainty expressed in the unorthodox direction. Those who showed a positive mean index of orthodoxy were classed as religious believers, those for whom it was negative as unbelievers. No significant difference was, however, found between the mean indices of certainty for the believers and the unbelievers. This result suggests the falsity of the common opinion that the principal alternative to religious orthodoxy is scepticism. In this group, at any rate, scepticism seemed to be uncommon, and the alternative to religious orthodoxy seemed to be equally dogmatic and convinced rejection of religious belief. There appeared to be no sex difference with respect to the tendency to certainty; there was no significant difference between the average degrees of certainty of the men and the women of the group tested. The women were, however, considerably more orthodox than the men.

The practical importance of such researches lies in the bearing they may have on the genesis of religious intolerance. The fact of the high degree of certainty attached to religious statements (whether in acceptance or rejection) indicates an irrational element in people's attitudes to religious propositions. If the strength of people's convictions were wholly determined by rational factors, such as the weighing of evidence, we should expect to find one generally accepted degree of conviction with some individuals feeling rather more or rather less convinced but with the frequency falling off in both directions from the generally accepted value. What we actually find is very different from this, many people express strong conviction of the truth of a proposition while many others are strongly convinced of its untruth.

This preference for a high degree of conviction is not, of course, found only in connection with religious propositions; it is found also for political beliefs. It may be surmised that the ground for it is the practical implications of such beliefs; they are not merely intellectual opinions but prescriptions for action. In the realm of action, it is often important to adopt one course or its opposite; we must drive a car to one side or the other of an obstacle; indeterminate or compromise action would lead to an accident. It is, therefore, not surprising that in such fields of thought as religion, we find that people tend to adopt high degrees of certainty, while the attitudes of scepticism and doubt tend to be unstable. This instability is, no doubt, part of the psychological explanation of sudden conversions to and from a religious attitude. Also the resulting tendency to high degrees of certainty may be surmised to be part of the explanation of the intolerance of doctrinal deviations that has led to religious persecutions.

If the tendency to certainty of religious belief has an obvious immediate advantage in increasing decisiveness of action, it has disadvantages in making difficult that suspension of judgment which is a pre-condition for rational decision; it also makes more difficult the understanding and tolerance of opinions that differ from one's own. The experimental demonstration of the psychological reality of the tendency to certainty does not imply that either this tendency or the intolerance that may result from it are unchangeable elements of human nature. If it is agreed that in irrationality and intolerance we are paying too high a price for decisiveness in action, the question of how they may be reduced becomes a problem in religious education.

Authoritarian methods of teaching religion can result in increase of religious certainty and of intolerance. These tendencies may even be reinforced by direct inculcation of hostile attitudes towards other religious groups. On the other hand, religious educators are not likely to be satisfied with an approach that leads to complete uncertainty and refusal to make a choice between one opinion and another. The problem would seem to be that of devising methods of developing the ability to accept one side of a controverted opinion while also understanding the reasonable grounds on which other people may hold the opposite view.

This necessity that the religious attitude should be able to combine definiteness of opinion with tolerance towards other opinions is one of the reasons for considering that the religious attitude should include an intellectual factor. It may be agreed that the intellectual factor cannot form the whole basis of religion; purely intellectual conviction of the reality of a spiritual world would be of little value unless it was associated with religious feelings and a religious system of motivation. But a religion based solely on feeling and the acceptance of a motivational system can easily develop into fanaticism. The habit of asking questions about one's religious beliefs which is introduced by the presence of an intellectual factor is a useful corrective to this danger of fanaticism.

REFERENCES

1. W. Trotter, *Instincts of the herd in peace and war*, London, 1916.
2. T. A. Ribot, *The psychology of the emotions* (Engl. trans.), London, 1897.
3. The Venerable Bede, *The ecclesiastical history of the English nation* (reprinted in Everyman Library), London, 1910.
4. I. B. Horner (Trans.), *Majjima-Nikaya (The middle length sayings)*, vol. II, no. 63, London, 1957.
5. R. H. Thouless, 'The tendency to certainty in religious belief', *British Journal of Psychology*, XXVI, Cambridge, 1935, pp. 16–31.
6. L. B. Brown, 'A study of religious belief'. *British Journal of Psychology*, LIII, Cambridge, 1962, pp. 259–72.

# 10. Religion and psychotherapy

One of the events that influenced the psychological approach to religion in the first half of the present century was the development by Sigmund Freud of Vienna of the psychotherapeutic method called 'psychoanalysis' and of the system of thought derived from this method. Both the practice and the theory came originally from Freud's curative work with patients suffering from the minor mental disorders classed as 'psychoneuroses'. These include hysteria with its mentally caused symptoms simulating such organic disorders as paralysis, anaesthesia, or digestive troubles, unreasonable anxieties and fears, and various compulsive actions. Although this work was the origin of Freud's psychoanalytic method and its accompanying theory, its implications were considered to extend far more widely. It was generally felt that the theory of psychoanalysis provided a key which could open the doors to a fuller understanding of human behaviour in a number of fields, including that of religion.

The essential point about Freud's curative method was that he got his patients to talk freely and without inhibitions about their problems so that the previously unknown causes of these problems might, under the guidance of the analyst, become apparent to the patient. The system of ideas and motives which influenced the patient's behaviour but was initially unrecognised by him was called the system of 'the unconscious'. The causes of the patient's illness were regarded by Freud as lying in the unconscious, and the curative value of psychoanalysis was considered to result from its causing what was hitherto unconscious to become conscious. When the causes of his illness became apparent to the patient he was able to deal with them in a conscious and rational manner.

The idea that some of the mental factors producing behaviour might lie outside the region of consciousness was not a new one but the idea that the road to the cure of mental illness might lie in the making conscious of the unconscious was new. So also was Freud's idea that a system of ideas might become unconscious by an active process of extrusion from the field of consciousness. This process was called by him 'repression'. He regarded neurotic disorders as a result of the repression of mental material that was painful, that is 'alarming or disagreeable or shameful by the standards of the subject's personality'.[1] Freud considered that such repressed mental material did not lose its power of influencing behaviour, but, since it was unconscious, it was outside the rational control of the patient and influenced his behaviour in irrational ways leading to the pathological behaviour of the neurotic disorder.

In Freud's own development of psychoanalytic theory, the main contribution to this repressed material was supposed to be made by the sexual system of instincts with their emotions of love, jealousy, and hatred. This system was considered to start in childhood, and, in the boy child, to take the typical form of the 'Oedipus complex', a passionate and possessive love of the mother coupled with a jealous hatred of the father. The adjustment to adult life was supposed to be accompanied by a repression of this emotional system as incompatible with the standards of the grown-up personality. Failure to accomplish this new adult adjustment might lead to neurosis. The non-neurotic person was also regarded by Freud as repressing his infantile sexuality and for him too it would remain an unconscious driving force behind his behaviour, which, however, might be directed towards some socially useful activity. Such redirection was called by Freud 'sublimation'.

To understand Freud's thought on this matter correctly, it is necessary to realise that he did not regard the repression of such instinctive forces as sexuality as necessarily a bad thing. It might lead to such bad results as neurotic disturbances, but it might also lead to socially constructive behaviour if these instinctive forces were successfully sublimated to socially useful ends. He was not in favour of the general liberation of instinctive forces; he regarded their repression as an essential factor in the building up of civilization.

If psychoanalytic theory had remained merely an attempt to explain the origins of neurotic illness, it would have no particular bearing on the psychology of religion. Freud, however, regarded it as having a much wider function than this, and applied the theory of repression to explain human behaviour that would not generally be classed as neurotic, including religious behaviour. The difference between neurotic persons and non-neurotic was not attributed by Freud to a difference in the contents of their unconscious but to the fact that 'neurotics break down at the same difficulties that are successfully overcome by normal people'. This view obviously leads to an extended view of the role of the unconscious and one may gain new understanding of the forces behind religious behaviour by considering how far they can be attributed to the sublimation of repressed emotional systems.

Freud's own first contribution to the psychology of religion was a speculation as to the origin of the primitive religion of totemism,[2] in which the being that is treated with reverence is an animal from which the clan claims to be descended. Normally the totem animal was sacred and could not be killed, but once a year there was a totem feast at which a totem animal was killed and eaten. Freud explained this as a result of the unconscious hostility to the father which he called the *Oedipus complex*, and supposed that the young men of a primal horde had killed their father in order to possess his wives. Freud's theory was that 'the totem-feast was the commemoration of the fearful deed from which sprang man's sense of guilt (or 'original sin') and which was the beginning at once of social organization, of religion and of ethical restriction'. Although Freud considered that the higher religions had developed from totemism, he adopted a somewhat different principle of explanation for this development. His contribution to speculation about the psychological origins of the higher religions is to be found in his later book: *The future of an illusion*.[3] He used the word 'illusion' to stand for a belief system based on human wishes but he pointed out that such a basis did not necessarily imply that the system was false. He did, in fact, believe that the religious system of ideas was false, not because it was based on wishes but rather because he believed that it had no other support. He believed that it had served a useful purpose, providing security in a hostile environment and a buttress for civilisation, but it appeared to him that this buttress could no longer serve the needs of modern man, who must replace it by reasonable grounds for living a civilised life. He regarded religion as an interim social neurosis out of which man must grow by education for reality.

This view of religion does not owe much to psychoanalytic theory. As Freud himself pointed out, most of it had been said before by non-believers in religion. Freud does not seem to support the frequently held view that the psychoanalytic point of view is necessarily destructive of the theoretical basis of the religious attitude, but rather held that this basis is known to be unsound anyway and that the task of psychoanalysis is to explain why, in spite of the unsoundness of its theoretical foundations, the religious attitude is so widely held. The religious believer will not necessarily differ from Freud in his account of the psychological origins of religion. He will certainly not object to the view that a system of thought cannot be accepted merely because it satisfies our needs; he will differ from Freud in his judgment that there are no rational grounds for holding a religious faith.

There is also a more extreme view of the necessarily destructive effect of psychoanalytic theory on religious faith which is often put forward by Freud's followers although not by Freud himself. This is the opinion that religious belief is shown to be untrue by the demonstration that it might be a product of the unconscious wishes of the person holding it. This is obviously inadequate as a ground for rejecting religious belief. The possibility that there might be an unconscious origin for a belief does not show that that belief is untrue, it merely shows that the truth of the belief cannot be inferred from the fact of people holding it. One could also speculate on the unconscious wishes and needs that are satisfied by the monarchy; the question of whether there is in a particular country a king or a queen who satisfies these needs would remain a separate one, to be decided by other considerations.

The apparent force of the case against religion based on the possibility of a psychoanalytic explanation of the origins of a religious attitude is reduced by the consideration that the argument can be used as well the other way round to demonstrate the psychoanalytic origins of unbelief. This was done by Rümke in his book *The psychology of unbelief.*[4] The standard Freudian treatment of religion is to treat unbelief as the normal attitude to religion and to ask what unconscious forces lead people to belief; Rümke, on the contrary, took religious belief as the normal attitude and asked what unconscious forces drive men to unbelief. This is a proper question. and psychoanalysis may provide at least a partial answer to it. If. however, this were regarded as an argument in defence of religious faith. it would suffer from the same defect as the psychoanalytic argument against religion already discussed. It may provide a psychological explanation of why men do not believe in religion; it cannot be a ground for deciding whether or not they are right to do so.

The Swiss pastor, Oscar Pfister, was one of those who found the psychoanalytic theory, even in its Freudian form, not incompatible with religious faith.[5] Although he rejected the materialism and agnosticism of Freud, it seemed to him that psychoanalysis provided answers to many of the questions that current theological teaching failed to answer. He considered that Christianity, which had started as a means of liberating men from fear and of releasing their love, had followed a course in which these aims had been lost sight of. It seemed rather to have produced fear and hatred. Pfister recognised that psychoanalysis was, like religion, on the side of love, and he said that when he applied its insights to his pastoral work, he found to his joy that he could 'discover facts and render help in a way which since then has not failed'.

In the early days of psychoanalysis there was a widespread expectation that it would prove to be a universal solvent of religious faith. This expectation has clearly not been fulfilled; experience has shown that people can be psychoanalysed and retain their religious faith; what they may be expected to shed in the course of their analysis is not their faith but some of their fanaticism. The importance of the unconsciousness of some of the roots of religious belief lies in the fact that they cannot be rationally examined by the person holding them so that he is led to an irrational degree of certainty about them and to an irrational hostility to any alternative belief system that seems to threaten them. The melancholy history of religious intolerance with its holy wars and burnings of heretics gives good grounds for welcoming any factor which helps to reduce this irrationality. If the understanding of the unconscious determination of religious opinions leads those influenced by psychoanalysis to be more charitable in judging the religious opinions of other people and more modest in maintaining their own, this is an unquestionable gain to religion.

Jung was a writer in the psychoanalytic tradition who adopted a more positive attitude towards religion than did Freud. Jung started as a disciple of Freud but diverged from him for various reasons including the fact that he thought Freud over-emphasised the part played by sex in the instinctual life of man. He extended the conception of the unconscious beyond Freud's personal unconscious that is made up of repressed memories of early life to include also a 'collective unconscious', based on the shared experiences of primitive man and acquired by the individual partly from tradition and partly by biological inheritance.[6] This collective unconscious was regarded by Jung as containing primordial images or 'archetypes', which are primitive symbols that may occur in dreams or visions and may be the basis of the religious ideas which are found to be common to many religions. Examples of such archetypal religious ideas given by Jung are: the suffering God-man, the trinity, the virgin birth, etc. Jung was at one with Freud in his view that the conscious acceptance of the repressed unconscious elements of the personality was a necessary part of the road to mental health. These repressed elements are what Jung calls the 'shadow side' of the personality. In his view, it is only when we have accepted our shadow side as far as we can, that we become fully developed personalities and can attain that attitude of unprejudiced objectivity which enables us to get in touch with the needs of others in mental distress.

Although he was far from being an orthodox Christian, Jung was much less negative in his attitude towards religion than was Freud. To him, the development of a religious attitude was a step to mental health. He said:

Among all my patients in the second half of life – that is to say, over thirty-five – there has not been one whose problem in the last resort was not that of finding a religious outlook on life. It is safe to say that every one of them fell ill because he had lost that which the living religions of every age have given to their followers, and none of them has been really healed who did not regain his religious outlook.[7]

This opinion is based on his own wide clinical experience and therefore deserves serious consideration. It must be admitted, however, that it lacks objective confirmation. A statistical test of this hypothesis would not be easy. It could not be tested simply by trying to discover whether there is a correlation between mental health and degree of acceptance of a religious attitude, since such correlation might be expected to be disturbed if those deficient in mental health were inclined to turn to religion as a method of healing. It would be necessary that it should be tested by a series of case histories sufficiently large and sufficiently representative to show whether or not in the life history of individuals the movement towards a religious adjustment was accompanied by a movement towards mental health. Such research has not yet been carried out.

On the level of clinical opinion, however, Jung's judgment has received support from another Swiss psychotherapist, Alphonse Maeder.[8] Maeder, at the beginning, rejected all forms of religion, but the difficulties of his patients led him to become concerned with the problems of religion and he was converted to the Christian faith. He reported that he then found himself better able to help his patients since he could guide them in the spiritual readjustments necessary for the restoration of their mental health.

A further development of the same line of thought is to be found in the work of Dr Frankl who has developed a system of psychotherapy which, in his own words, 'not only recognizes man's spirit, but actually starts from it'.[9] He quotes research findings which indicate that about twenty per cent of neuroses result from the inability of the patients to find any purpose in life. It may be the task of the therapist to direct them to a meaning in life by the realisation of some value. This realisation may be achieved, not only by accomplishing worthwhile tasks, but also sometimes by the adoption of an attitude of acceptance of inevitable suffering.

Such medical ministry may have to be accomplished by the doctor who is attending the patient. It would seem however, to be especially the function of the religious pastor who can offer to members of his flock a religious attitude which gives meaning to their lives.

This would imply some overlapping of the work of the medical psychotherapist and that of the religious pastor. The psychotherapist may find spiritual problems in his patients' lives with which he feels that he is incompetent to deal, while the pastor may be consulted by members of his flock who show a degree of mental disturbance which is beyond his skill. The practical solution of this difficulty would seem to be mutual cooperation rather than that either party should seek to master the skills of the other. Certainly the religious pastor could be trained in the technique of psychoanalysis; so trained there is no reason why he should not be as skilled a psychoanalyst as a doctor with the same training. But the attitude of objective acceptance, necessary in the attitude of a psychotherapist to his patient, may not be appropriate to the pastor. In his pastoral work, he deals with sin and with conflicts on the conscious level. If the religious pastor adopted towards the moral problems of his flock the attitude of indifference towards right and wrong implied in the psychotherapist's 'objective acceptance', they might well feel that his attitude was not meeting their needs.

The contribution that the religious pastor can make to the mental problems of his patients would seem to be not that made by a relatively unskilled psychotherapist but that which can be made by a highly skilled spiritual ministry (in Frankl's sense of the word 'ministry'). The pastor should be able to direct those who find life meaningless to an attitude which gives a meaning to life. This attitude may be that of a religious acceptance of suffering and frustration. Jung reports that, when he faces such problems, the modern man goes to his medical adviser rather than to a religious pastor. May this be a result of the fact that such pastoral skill is too little developed in the training of religious ministers, at least in some denominations? The religious pastor may be helped to appreciate the difficulties of those who need his spiritual advice if he realises that some of these difficulties may have unconscious roots. Without himself trying to acquire the techniques of uncovering these roots, it may be as well that he should have sufficient understanding of the psychotherapist's work to be able to advise the more unbalanced members of his flock when they need the services of a psychotherapist. He may be able in this way to serve his flock better than he could by himself undertaking the psychotherapist's role.

It may be the case, as Jung believed, that the achievement of mental health results from the adoption of a religious attitude. It remains true that, from the point of view of the religious person, this is not the aim of religion. For the religious believer, God and the spiritual world are realities, and the adoption of a proper attitude towards them cannot be regarded by him as merely a device to achieve freedom from neurotic disturbance. If he believes that the proper end of man is to love and serve God, he regards this service and love as an end in itself, not as a means to promote peace of mind. If tranquillity and mental health come from an attitude of acceptance of spiritual realities, this is a good which the religious man may accept gratefully; it is not the end for which his religious attitude exists.

## REFERENCES

1. S. Freud, *An autobiographical study* (Engl. trans.), London, 1935.
2. S. Freud, *Totem and taboo* (Engl. trans.), New York, 1918.
3. S. Freud, *The future of an illusion* (Engl. trans.), London, 1928.
4. H. C. Rümke, *The psychology of unbelief* (Engl. trans.), London, 1952.
5. O. Pfister, *Christianity and fear* (Engl. trans.), London, 1948.
6. C. G. Jung, *Psychology and religion*, New Haven, 1938.
7. C. G. Jung, *Modern man in search of a soul*, London, 1933.
8. A. Maeder, *Ways to psychic health* (Engl. trans.), London, 1954.
9. V. E. Frankl, *The doctor and the soul* (Engl. trans.), London, 1965.

# 11. Psychical research and religion

One of the branches of psychology which is generally considered to be closely linked with religion is that which has been called 'psychical research' or (more recently) 'parapsychology'. This is the attempt to study scientifically such topics as the supposed transference of thought from one mind to another without sensory communication, the foretelling of the future, ostensible communication with the departed in mediumistic seances, the movement of objects without contact, and so on. All these topics involve events that may be classed as 'paranormal'. The use of this term implies that such events are unusual or unexpected. It does not necessarily imply that any such events really take place; that is a question which has to be answered by the results of research. Although much remains unclear, research has to a great extent answered the basic question as to whether such paranormal events ever take place. It appears that they do and that any complete view of the world must take into account such occurrences. The conditions and limitations of their occurrence are less clear, nor do we know whether they are as exceptional as they seem to be or whether paranormal events of a less striking kind are taking place all the time.

The importance for religious thinking of the recognition of the reality of the paranormal is perhaps somewhat less than was often supposed by the early founders of the Society for Psychical Research in the last half of last century. Some of these felt that the traditional foundations for religious faith had been undermined by the advances of science and that a new scientifically based religion might be built on the foundations of psychical research. No experimental study, however, can deal directly with the central elements of religious faith: the existence of God, the duty of love, or the meaningfulness of human life, although there are a number of other questions of concern to religious thought on which psychical research can be expected to throw light.

The most important question would seem to be whether the universe appears to be of such a nature that it would not be unreasonable to suppose that it had a spiritual component. It was an obvious implication of Victorian scientific thought (though not accepted by all Victorian scientists) that, when one had described the material universe and its causal interconnections, one had said all about the world that could meaningfully be said. This view might be expressed as that of regarding the material universe as a closed system. Although men might not know all about this system at any particular time, it was supposed that what remained to be found out was finite, that in principle everything could be known by continuing the same process of finding out, and that everything so discovered would be of the same kind as what was already known.

There is much in the present research position, even in the physical sciences, which throws doubt on this simple picture of a body of scientific knowledge which only needs completion along existing lines. More doubt is thrown on it by well-attested results of psychical research. For example, neither the facts of communication without sensory interchange (extra-sensory perception or ESP) nor those of movement of objects without contact (psycho-kinesis or PK) seem to be capable of explanation in terms of the kind of physical laws with which orthodox science is familiar. Yet the reality of these things has been well demonstrated by careful experiment as well as by much observation of spontaneous cases.[1] There seems to be a region of reality of a very different kind from that explored by the physical and biological sciences. If this is accepted, it cannot be supposed to prove the reality of the spiritual world postulated by the religions but it does leave open the possibility of a spiritual world and of a God, whereas these possibilities had seemed to be closed by the world view of Victorian science. Psychical research provides one of the indications that the universe is such that a religious view of it is not unreasonable. Whether we decide that such a religious view is a true one is likely to be determined only in part by considerations drawn from psychical research.

This question about the nature of the universe is, no doubt, the most important one on which psychical research can throw light. There are also more peripheral questions of concern to religious faith that can be investigated by the methods of psychical research: whether human consciousness goes on after bodily death, whether the reported religious miracles are events of a kind that can ever take place, whether prophecy is a possibility, and what is the status of the visions and apparitions which are often accepted as possessing some kind of spiritual reality by those experiencing them.

On the question of the possibility of human consciousness surviving death, there is an obvious conflict between the teachings of most religions and the commonly accepted opinion based on scientific habits of thought that expects extinction of consciousness at death. The expectation of extinction is based on the view that consciousness is simply a property of such complex organic systems as the human brain, and that, when such a system suffers death and dissolution, the associated stream of consciousness necessarily comes to an end. It would be a mistake to suppose that this opinion of non-survival has been proved by any scientific observation on the relation of consciousness to nervous systems. It must rather be regarded as a habit of thought which results from observations of correlations between conscious experiences and neurological events such as the production of perceptual experiences by electrical stimulation of the cerebral cortex and the disappearance of all experience when the nervous system suffers from concussion.

The bearing of physical research on this problem is two-fold. First, its results seem to indicate a view of human consciousness as something other than a mere by-product of nervous activity, thus weakening the expectation that conscious experience must come to an end when at death the nervous system ceases to function. Secondly, there is the more direct evidence given by ostensible communications from the spirits of those who have died, and by the observation of conditions, called 'out of the body experiences' in which the stream of consciousness seems to be spatially distinct from the physical body. If consciousness is considered to be merely an aspect of the activity of a nervous system, it is reasonable to suppose that it will disappear when the activity of the nervous system comes to an end at the death of the body. Any fact incompatible with this explanation of consciousness though it may not in itself provide positive evidence of survival, weakens the case for this expectation of the disappearance of consciousness at bodily death. The occurrence of such events as telepathy, clairvoyance, precognition, and psycho-kinesis is generally recognised to be incompatible with the orthodox physical theory of consciousness. Because of this incompatibility, holders of that theory are inclined to deny strongly the reality of the whole class of paranormal events. There is, however, overwhelming evidence that at least some paranormal events do take place under the most rigorously controlled conditions. It follows that any theory of consciousness which would prohibit such events must be wrong, or, at least, incomplete. So arguments against survival based on the implications of the physical theory of consciousness become very dubious. The possibility is open that consciousness is a reality of its own kind. Consciousness in ourselves as living organisms is at present closely bound up with the activity of a nervous system, but it is possible that it may be able to continue independently when the nervous system has come to an end after bodily death.

The primary meaning of survival after death is that the stream of consciousness goes on after bodily death. This, however, cannot be directly verified for other persons than oneself. When I die I may have the experience of finding that my consciousness continues although my body is dead. I cannot have any corresponding experience about the continuance after death of the stream of consciousness of any other person. Any evidence brought forward for the survival of another must be of the indirect kind provided by the survival of some characteristic of their personality or of a recognisable part of their memory system. A conscious survival that was not accompanied by any continuity of personality or of memory would be, in principle, unverifiable. The situation generally regarded as providing a test of the survival of the personalities or memories of those who have died is the mediumistic seance. In a typical seance messages ostensibly from the dead are received through an individual who is called a 'medium'. The medium may be in a state of trance or in ordinary waking consciousness; messages may be received by the medium's own speech, or through automatic writing or in various other ways. The type of evidence that is felt by sitters to point to the identity of the communicator may be 'recognition' when the character of the message received (even sometimes the intonation of the communicating voice) are felt to be unmistakeably characteristic of the deceased individual. This kind of evidence can be of compelling force to the person experiencing it but it is not easily submitted to any process of objective verification. A more easily communicable kind of evidence is that provided by the communicator producing some kind of identifying information that would be known to the deceased person but not to anyone present at the seance. Subsequent verification of the information provides evidence that the source was the deceased person, although this conclusion may be avoided by attributing the information to the telepathic powers of the medium.

Various ways have been devised for avoiding this alternative explanation by telepathy. The cross-correspondences, in which parts of a total message were communicated by different mediums, have been claimed to be inexplicable by any process of telepathy from the living.[1] This may be so but the cross-correspondences are difficult to evaluate. A simpler method would be one in which a selected bit of information is provided by the intending communicator during his lifetime. If mediums cannot obtain this information during the lifetime of the intending communicator it can reasonably be inferred that its discovery is beyond their telepathic powers. If then it comes through mediums easily after his death, when he is intending to communicate it, this fact will point very strongly to the surviving communicator as the source of the information. Experiments of this type are being carried out; in one of them the information to be communicated is the key to a cipher,[3] in another it is the setting of a combination lock.[4] These experiments are still only in an early stage, so nothing can yet be said of how successful they will prove to be. In the meantime, we must judge the strength of the empirical evidence for survival from the best of the existing mediumistic communications, as, for example, the 'Palm Sunday' case[5] and the 'Tennant' communications through Geraldine Cummins.[6] In these and many other cases, the evidence for some communication from deceased personalities seems too strong to be easily dismissed as merely the result of telepathic or ESP powers of the mediums. On the other hand, whatever other ingredients such communications may have, they seem to be heavily diluted by material derived from the medium's own mind or from the minds of the sitters, and we have no reliable means of separating the genuine elements of communication from these extraneous factors. It follows that, although seances may give strong indications of the survival of some elements of personality after the death of the body, there is no good reason for regarding them as reliable guides to the character of a future life; statements on such matters may reflect the opinions of the medium or of the sitters.

Persons committed to a religious point of view are often impatient of the evidence produced at seances as being remote from the questions that interest them. Obviously the mere demonstration of the fact of survival would fall far short of a demonstration of what a Christian means by 'eternal life'. Yet the survival of personality is one of the facts entailed by the conception of eternal life, and a scientific confirmation of survival helps to make credible the fuller conception of eternal life. The mere acceptance of survival would not perhaps carry anyone very far towards a religious faith; those oppressed with the futility of life will find no consolation in the idea of that futility going on for ever. For many persons, however, the acceptance of the survival of death may be a first step towards a religious faith.

Another direction in which psychical research has bearings on religion is in the field of the alleged miraculous happenings which are reported as incidents in the lives of great religious figures and which seem to have been regarded by their contemporaries as evidence of the spiritual stature of these figures. An example is to be found in the reports of miraculous events (or 'signs') in the New Testament. These (with the possible exception of the miracles of healing) are now commonly supposed to be rather misleading accounts of natural events which are not evidence of anything supernatural about Jesus Christ. Psychical research suggests the possibility of a different view. A reported miracle may not be a mistaken report of a natural event but a substantially correct report of a paranormal event. Such paranormal events may have taken place with unusual frequency in connection with Jesus Christ and his immediate disciples and they may have been correctly interpreted by his contemporaries as signs of something remarkable in Jesus himself.[7]

The 'signs' that are reported in the New Testament are of various kinds. Some are events of a physical order such as the feeding of the five thousand. Psychical research does little to remove the difficulties of these except to show that paranormal events of a physical order can take place under laboratory conditions.[8] These certainly do not as yet include the multiplication of food although this too is more commonly reported in religious history than one might expect.[9]

Miracles of healing are more easily accepted since some, at least, of these may be explained by the normal psychological process of suggestic•. There may also be a genuinely paranormal healing power exercised by some individuals although it is difficult to make a scientifically certain discrimination between this possibility and the alternative explanation by suggestion.

Another class of miraculous events in the New Testament is that in which Jesus was reported to have shown paranormal knowledge of events or of other people's thoughts. This is the capacity known as extra-sensory perception (ESP) or telepathy. There is abundant evidence, both spontaneous and experimental, of the reality of this capacity and of its considerable development in some gifted individuals.[10] Psychical research has not indeed demonstrated any correlation between this capacity and the spiritual development of its possessor although there is some spontaneous evidence of such a correlation; the dimension of holiness is not one that has yet been explored by psychical research.

An example of extra-sensory knowledge displayed by Jesus was that of the woman of Samaria who was told that she had five husbands and was then living with a man who was not her husband and is reported to have replied: 'Sir, I perceive that you are a prophet'. later developing this to the suggestion that he might be 'the Christ' (John 4. 19 and 29). A similar reaction is reported by Nathanael to the statement by Jesus that he had already seen him under a fig-tree: 'Rabbi, you are the Son of God. You are the King of Israel' (John 1.49). There are also references to Jesus knowing the thoughts of his Pharisee critics in Matt. 3.25, and of his quarrelling disciples in Luke 9.47, and a more general reference to his unusual ESP powers in John 2.25 where it is said that he 'knew all men, and needed no one to bear witness to man'. Similar paranormal events are reported in the lives of other leading religious figures, both Christian and non-Christian. For example, ESP is reported in the New Testament of John the Baptist (Matt. 3.14) and of St Peter (Acts 5.3). There are many examples from more recent times, such as that of the Curé d'Ars who was said to be able 'to read a man's heart like an open book' and apparently owed his reputation as an unusually skilled confessor partly to this gift.[11]

Outside the Christian tradition we also find that leading religious figures are credited with paranormal powers including ESP and that those powers were regarded as evidence of their holiness. It is, for example, reported of the Buddha that when a certain hermit did not want him to be present at a sacrifice, the Buddha, understanding this 'by the power of his mind' did not go to the hermit that evening.[12] It is recorded that when the hermit knew that this was why the Buddha had not come, he concluded that the Buddha had great faculties but still refused to believe that the Buddha was holy like himself. It was only as a result of the Buddha performing many miracles of this kind that the hermit became his disciple. A more recent example from India is that of the nineteenth-century holy man Sri Ramakrishna,[13] of whom it was said that he could 'read a man's inmost thought'. His biographer records a number of cases in which he is said to have answered objections to what he was saying when these objections had been merely thought and not expressed.

In some religious traditions such paranormal occurrences, whether of ESP, of healing or of some physical event, are often regarded as evidence of the holiness of the person producing the event. This is not a common opinion in our own culture although we ought to be ready to consider it as a possible one; it is still widely held in India. The comments of the witnesses of the miracles of Jesus show that they shared this opinion and considered the miracles as signs that he might be the Messiah. It seems also that Jesus Christ himself endorsed this opinion. Thus when he received a query from John the Baptist as to whether he was the one that should come, the first part of his reply was a reference to the miracles: 'Go and tell John what you have seen and heard: the blind receive their sight, the lame walk . . . the dead are raised up.' (Luke 7.22). Although in many religious traditions there is an opinion that paranormal powers may be a mark of holy persons, there may also be in the same traditions an opinion that they can be the mark of an unholy person. In the Middle Ages, saints were supposed to have paranormal powers, but so also were sorcerers, the latter using their powers for evil ends. In New Testament times too, this ambiguity of paranormal signs seems to have been accepted. Thus the Pharisees are reported to have suggested that Jesus cast out devils by the power of Beelzebub (Matt. 12.24). A similar view seems to be implied by the report of Simon the magician who produced paranormal phenomena which led many to regard him as 'that power of God which is called Great' (Acts 8.11). Calling Simon a 'magician' seems to imply that his paranormal phenomena were regarded as genuine but of evil origin.

This view of the connection between holiness and the production of paranormal events may be expressed by saying that paranormal phenomena were regarded as signs that the person producing them differed from other men in the dimension of holiness either in a positive or a negative direction. Whether the person with paranormal powers was regarded as holy or unholy depended partly on whether he used those powers for the good of others or for selfish and anti-social ends, partly by the total impression of what he did and said. These criteria showed that Jesus and the Buddha and Sri Ramakrishna varied from the normal in the direction of goodness. The paranormal events reported of these religious figures were taken as signs of something beyond goodness which may be expressed in various ways in various religious traditions: a 'holy man', a 'son of God', a 'fully enlightened one' or an 'incarnation of God'.

The actual occurrence of any miracle by a particular religious figure is, of course, subject to all the uncertainty of the ways in which they have been recorded. Psychical research cannot guarantee the reality of any particular past miracle; it does, however, remove the additional ground for disbelief arising from the conviction that such events are intrinsically impossible. It allows us to read such religious narratives as the Gospels and the Acts of the Apostles with our minds open to the possibility that some, at least, of the miracles described may have taken place, and that their observation of these signs of holiness may have been one of the reasons why the disciples of Jesus accepted him as their master and lord.

When ESP is studied experimentally, it is found to be a means of attaining knowledge not only of contemporary events but also of future events. Precognition or prophecy seems to be a paranormal possibility. So when we read in religious narratives of Joseph or Daniel foretelling future events by the interpretation of dreams, or of Jesus foretelling the destruction of Jerusalem, the assured results of psychical research forbid us to dismiss these events as impossibilities. That they were possible, does not, of course, imply that they really took place; this must be decided by other considerations. In general, it is obviously difficult to verify the success in foretelling of the future that was attained by prophecies in the past. It is often uncertain at what date the alleged prophecies were inserted into the documents in which they occur. It is also generally unclear to what particular series of events they were intended to refer. The fight between a lion and an eagle in the second book of Esdras, was, for example, claimed in 1914 to be a prophecy of the fighting between England and Germany that started that year. In 1939, it was regarded more plausibly as a prophecy of the Second World War, the three heads of the eagle representing Hitler, Göring and Goebbels. No doubt it had also been regarded as prophetic of earlier wars. The symbolic form in which prophecies are often couched also makes it difficult to judge how far they correspond with future events. Psychical research cannot remove any of these sources of uncertainty as to the fulfilment of past prophecies. What it does is to remove the obstacle to the acceptance of the reality of prophecy which arises from the conviction that non-inferential foretelling of the future is impossible. Prophecy too may be a paranormal power possessed by the holy ones, and accounts of prophecy and of fulfilments of prophecy in religious narratives should also be considered as elements that are possibly true.

Another point of contact between religion and psychical research is their common interest in visual appearances of the departed. The apparitions studied in psychical research may be either of living persons or of those who have died.[14] In both cases what is seen has the visual characteristics of a solid, living body, and may include such non-living material as clothes and perhaps a walking-stick.[15] In these respects, apparitions differ from the relatively formless ghosts of fiction. They are like living persons in appearance, but they do not move physical objects, may appear or disappear suddenly, and do not engage in the two-way communication of conversation although they may themselves say a few words. It has been argued that the absence of conversation and the presence of such non-living accessories as clothes, imply that the apparition cannot be regarded as a perceived object but rather as a mental creation of the perceiver, although the cause of his act of creation may be something outside himself. such as a telepathic influence coming from the deceased person.

The study of non-religious apparitions provides some criteria for the evaluation of religious appearances. When a religious vision shows the characteristics of sudden appearance and disappearance and absence of two-way communication and of any effects in the physical world, it may be regarded as belonging to the same class as the apparitions studied in psychical research. It may be supposed to be a creation of the perceptual process of the person perceiving it. although it must also be considered that the cause of this creation may be of a spiritual order. This may be a sufficient account of the appearance of the Virgin Mary to Bernadette. One may suppose that the Virgin Mary was not herself the object of Bernadette's perception without committing oneself to the opinion that she merely imagined the incident. The same may be true of St Paul's vision of Christ on the road to Damascus. Where, however, there is full two-way communication. and where there are physical effects (as was reported in the appearance of Jesus to his two disciples at Emmaus) we can say that the reported incident does not fit into the pattern of the typical apparition.

While the apparitions of deceased persons are not unknown in everyday life they may well occur more commonly in a religious setting. As in the case of miracles, the findings of psychical research tell against the common tendency to disbelieve automatically accounts of religious visions, and also against any tendency to suppose that these are necessarily what they are taken to be by the person experiencing them: actual presences in spiritual form of beings belonging to the spiritual world. They may be accepted as creations by the perceptual processes of the person perceiving them, without prejudice to the possibility that the causes of this creation may be of a spiritual order.

Psychical research (or parapsychology) is a growing science. Already it shows suggestive contacts with religious problems. It seems to make more plausible a point of view which includes a spiritual world and a life after death, and it seems to make more understandable such facts of religious narratives as miracles. prophecies, and visions. It seems likely that in the future it will throw more light on the problems of religion.

REFERENCES

1. J. B. Rhine and J. G. Pratt, *Parapsychology: frontier science of the mind*, Springfield (Ill.), 1957.
2. H. F. Saltmarsh, *Evidence of personal survival from cross-correspondences*, London, 1938.
3. R. H. Thouless, 'A test of survival' and 'Additional note on a test of survival', *Proceedings of the Society for Psychical Research*, XLVIII, 1948, pp. 253–63 and 342–3.
4. I. Stevenson, 'The combination lock test for survival', *Journal of the American Society for Psychical Research*, LXII, 1968, pp. 246–54.
5. Jean Balfour, 'The "Palm Sunday" case; new light on an old love story', *Proceedings of the Society for Psychical Research*, LII, 1960, pp. 79–267.
6. Geraldine Cummins, and Signe Toksvig, *Swan on a black sea*, London, 1965.
7. R. H. Thouless, 'Miracles and psychical research', *Theology*, LXXII, London, 1969, pp. 253–8.
8. Louisa E. Rhine, *Mind over matter*, New York and London, 1970.
9. H. Thurston, *The physical phenomena of mysticism*, London, 1952.
10. S. G. Soal and F. Bateman, *Modern experiments in telepathy*, London, 1954.
11. F. Trochu, *The Curè d'Ars: a shorter biography* (English trans.), London, 1955.
12. Max Muller (Ed.), 'Vinaya texts', *Sacred books of the East*, XIII, Oxford, 1881.
13. Swami Nikhilananda (Trans.), *The Gospel of Sri Ramakrishna*, Madras, 1944.
14. E. Gurney, F. W. H. Myers and F. Podmore, *Phantasms of the living*, London, 1886 (abridged version, New York, 1962).
15. G. N. M. Tyrrell, *Apparitions* (7th Myers Memorial Lecture), London, 1943, revd. edn. 1953.

# 12. The psychology of prayer

The word 'prayer' is sometimes used to mean only the activity of using words either publicly or privately for making petitions to a divine being. Writers on religion have, however, generally preferred to adopt a wider use of the word 'prayer'. They have used it to include not only the making of petitions but also the use of words addressed to divine beings in other ways and for non-verbal states of consciousness in which the mind is directed towards the spiritual world (in submission, or in love, or in worship). In public (or communal) prayer, the use of words is necessary since this is an activity involving social interaction. In private prayer also, vocal or inner speech may be used but the accounts given by many, of their own prayer practices, show that it may be dispensed with. The kind of prayer that does not involve any kind of verbalisation is often called 'mental prayer'. The wider use of the word 'prayer' will be adopted here; the particular kind of prayer in which petitions are made will be distinguished as 'petitionary prayer'.

In addition to prayer proper, there is a prayer-like religious activity which uses both verbal thinking and mental imagery. This differs from prayer in the fact that it is not primarily directed to the spiritual world but to modifying the state of consciousness or the behaviour patterns of the person engaged in it. This activity is 'meditation' which will be discussed in the next chapter. The distinction between these two kinds of religious mental activity is not, of course, a sharp one. Meditation may be more or less accompanied by the mental attitude of prayer; prayer may have more or less effect on the consciousness of the person praying. The psychologist may be more interested in such subjective effects of prayer than in the question of what consequences the prayer may have in the spiritual world, but these subjective effects of the prayer are not its primary purpose from the point of view of the person praying. It is, therefore, useful to make the distinction between 'prayer' in which the purpose is primarily objective and 'meditation' in which it is primarily subjective.

Prayer in its various forms is one of the principal activities of the religious life, and generally, although not always, petitionary prayer is an important part of prayer activity. Some religious people feel difficulty about the intellectual justification of petitionary prayer and are unable to find a way of thinking about the divine will which would accommodate the idea that that will was affected by human petitions. Petitionary prayer may then be increasingly replaced by the prayer of resignation to God's will. More commonly the offering of petitions is accepted as a natural reaction of the individual who believes in a personal God. He may not concern himself with the intellectual problems of the appropriateness of such a reaction.

Buddhism (at least in its primitive Theravada form) does not admit petitionary prayer amongst its religious practices. This is a necessary consequence of its teaching that everything that happens is in accordance with a system of laws from which the gods are not exempt. Although this is official Buddhist teaching, however, it seems that petitionary prayer does play a part in popular Buddhist practice. I have seen, in Ceylon, people crowding to pray in a Roman Catholic church. These, I was told, were not Christians but Buddhists who offered their petitions where they hoped they would be effective. Buddhist temples also commonly contain a shrine to a Hindu deity, and petitions are said to be addressed frequently to this deity although they would not be addressed to the Buddha. The psychological craving for the satisfaction given by petitionary prayer seems to be too strong amongst ordinary people to be suppressed by official discouragement. It is to be noted also that there are practices approved in Theravada Buddhist religious practice which are closely related to petitionary prayer. For example, Marie Byles, a solicitor of Sydney, who practised meditation at the Maha Bodhi meditation centre in Burma, describes how, after meditation, the meditant 'suffused all beings with loving kindness.'[1] It is not clear whether this exercise was regarded as having purely subjective effects by increasing the kindly sentiments of the meditant. If so it would be a meditational activity related to auto-suggestion. If, however, it were regarded as aimed at increasing the well-being of those on whom it was directed, it would be a prayer-like form of activity not essentially different from that of a member of a theistic religion who prays for the well-being of other men.

Those who use and value petitionary prayer in the religious traditions in which it is approved do not, of course, commonly suppose that in such prayer they have a source of spiritual power available for the attainment of their own personal ends. The business man who prayed for his own enrichment at the expense of his business rivals would generally be regarded as attempting an improper use of prayer, an attempt that, because improper, would also be ineffective.

Those who have shown the simplest faith in the efficacy of petitionary prayer have used it for altruistic ends that they regarded as of spiritual value. William James relates the case of George Müller, who built and maintained orphanages and fed a large number of people without holding any considerable sum of money or falling into debt. When there was no more food for his dependants, they prayed and the needed money came. A more recent similar case is that of David Wilkerson, a Pentecostalist minister who worked among the teen-age drug addicts of New York.[2] He too ran an institution without much capital in hand. On an occasion when there was no money for the day's food he gathered his staff and they prayed that food might be supplied. After this prayer had been going on for some time, a woman knocked at the door with the sum of money required for their food that day. Unlike Mr Müller, the Rev. D. Wilkerson did raise a mortgage on his building, but the first payment of $4,200 had to be made. For this sum Mr Wilkerson prayed and stated his needs to the congregation of the local church. His prayer included the request that the exact sum might be given although this required sum was not mentioned to the congregation. After the address members of the congregation came in and gave their individual contributions which totalled $4,400. It was only after completing the payment that Mr Wilkerson discovered that there were also legal expenses of $200 which he had not allowed for in his original estimate of the amount required.

Such expectation of detailed fulfilment of petitionary prayers, even for altruistic and religious ends, is somewhat exceptional. More commonly petitionary prayer is accompanied by prayer of submission to the divine will. Its reward is then not detailed fulfilment but the relaxation of tension which results from the conviction that the matter prayed about is left in the hands of God.

A simple variant of petitionary prayer is the impersonal expression of a wish which is described by Rivers as the characteristic form of communal prayer amongst the Todas, an Indian people whose activity is centred round their dairies.[3] These prayers do not take the form of supplications to a deity; a typical example is: 'May it be well with the buffaloes and calves, may there be no disease, may there be no destroyer ... may clouds rise, may grass flourish, may water spring'. The prayer ended with the names of gods or sacred objects followed by the word *idith* 'for the sake of'. This is clearly a prayer of the petitionary kind although not in the form of a petition addressed to a god. In form it is more like the Buddhist practice of projecting loving kindness on all beings. Nor is this grammatical structure unknown in Christian prayer although it is less common than the form of supplication. It is, however, to be found in the early clauses of the Lord's Prayer: 'Hallowed be thy name. Thy kingdom come. Thy will be done'. It is also used in the well-known prayer for the departed: 'May the souls of the faithful, by the mercy of God, rest in peace.' Ducasse has suggested that the Todas form of prayer may be more primitive than that of petition addressed to a person, that the beginning of prayer may be simply the articulation of a wish fervent enough to lead to utterance.[4] Rivers himself seemed more inclined to think that these prayers were the surviving part of what were once communal petitions to personal deities belonging to a now forgotten mythology. However this may be, it is interesting to note that petitionary prayer may take a linguistic form other than that of supplication to a divine being.

Although petitionary prayer is only one of many varieties of prayer, which also include praise, thanksgiving, submission, etc., it is one of the most characteristic forms of prayer and is naturally the first to attract the attention of psychologists concerned with the empirical study of religion. The problem with which these are concerned is not, of course, that of how far petitionary prayer has a measurable effect on the events of the outside world. It is true that many years ago, Galton suggested an experiment in which prayers for rain should be made over one half of England while prayers for fine weather were made over the other half, and that the rainfall measurements of the two halves should be compared statistically in order to discover whether there was a significant difference between them.[5]

This experiment does not differ in principle from that reported in the Book of Judges to have been carried out by Gideon when he prayed on successive nights for his fleece to be wet with dew while the surrounding ground was dry, and for the ground to be wet with dew and the fleece dry. Galton's experiment would not, however, be a psychological one; it might rather be classified as belonging to experimental theology. The psychologist's concern is with a different set of questions, with how people think and behave with respect to petitionary prayer. A psychological enquiry may be directed towards discovering the extent to which petitionary prayer is practised and what those who practise it expect to be its results. An interesting question for the psychologist would be, for example, what religious believers would expect to be the result of Galton's experiment.

An enquiry concerned with children's ideas about prayer was made in Brussels by the Rev. A. Godin, S.J. and Sister Bernadette Van Roey.[6] This was particularly directed towards the study of the element in children's religious thought that has been called 'animism' which interprets physical events in terms appropriate only to living beings. This investigation used the technique of enquiry originated by Piaget in which stories embodying imaginary situations are presented to the child who is then asked to make comments on them, or to reply to specific questions about them. For example, one of the stories used by Godin and Van Roey was of a child who broke a vase and prayed that her parents would not find out that she had done it. When the father came home a gust of wind came into the house as he opened the door, and when he found the vase broken he supposed that it was by this gust. The psychological problem with which the investigators were concerned was that of how a child who read this story interpreted the occurrence of the gust which led to this mistake and how he supposed it to be related to the child's prayer that her own responsibility for the breakage would not be discovered. They found that replies to such questions showing an animistic type of thinking in the subjects rose to a maximum at 12 years of age, afterwards decreasing. They considered that such animistic thinking may be partly primitive, but that it may also be partly the product of the child's religious education. The practical implication of such enquiries is to suggest the desirability of weeding out from religious education such elements as lead to over-simplified ideas on religious topics which will, in any case, have to be discarded in the attainment of a mature religious attitude.

Another investigation concerned with petitionary prayer was made by Professor L. Brown and myself.[7] Our subjects were 181 schoolgirls of various faiths from two secondary schools in Adelaide (South Australia). They were told certain stories involving the practice of petitionary prayer in various situations (varying in degree of self-involvement and in moral quality of the end prayed for). After each story they were questioned on two points: the expected 'causal efficacy' of the prayer (its expected effect on the course of events) and its appropriateness (whether the girl thought that such prayer should have been offered in that situation).

The main finding was that belief in the causal efficacy of petitionary prayer declined considerably with increasing age (from 35 per cent at age 12–13 to 19 per cent at age 16–17), while there was no corresponding decrease in the belief in the appropriateness of petitionary prayer (51 per cent at age 12–13 and 48 per cent at age 16–17). It looks as if a simple view of prayer as an effective means of obtaining results in the world outside decreases as the children grow older, but they retain approval of the practice of petitionary prayer, increasingly finding its justification on grounds other than the expectation that it will alter the course of events.

It is evident that many of the questions that one would be inclined to ask about prayer cannot be answered by any psychological method of investigation. There are, however, also a number of questions which could be but have not yet been so answered; the investigations mentioned above are only a beginning of systematic enquiry in this field. Further investigations along similar lines may provide us with more information about prayer beliefs and practices which could help in the understanding of the religious situation and could be a guide to those responsible for religious training.

REFERENCES

1. Marie B. Byles, *Journey into Burmese silence*, London, 1962.
2. D. Wilkerson, *The cross and the switchblade*, London, 1963.
3. W. H. R. Rivers, *The Todas*, London, 1906.
4. C. J. Ducasse, *A philosophical scrutiny of religion*, New York, 1953.

5. Francis Galton, *Inquiries into human faculty and its development,* London, 1883 (reprinted Everyman's Library, 1907).

6. A. Godin and Bernadette Van Roey, 'Immanent justice and divine protection in children of 6 to 14 years', *Lumen Vitae,* xiv, Brussels, 1959, pp. 129–48.

7. R. H. Thouless and L. B. Brown, 'Petitionary prayer: belief in its appropriateness and causal efficacy among adolescent girls', in *From religious experience to a religious attitude* (Ed. A. Godin), Brussels, 1964.

# 13. The psychology of meditation

In contrast with prayer, which is essentially directed towards God or towards a divine being, there is the closely related activity of meditation which is primarily directed towards producing spiritual results on the person meditating. As has already been pointed out, there is no sharp distinction between these two types of activity. A mental activity ostensibly directed towards the spiritual world has effects also on the state of consciousness of the person engaged in it; a prayer activity may, for example, reduce mental tension and replace it by peace of mind. Equally, meditation may contain an element of prayer and may be a prayer-like activity. Yet, although the division is not sharp, we may conveniently make a rough distinction between meditation which is primarily subjective in its reference, and prayer which is primarily objective.

On its psychological side, discursive meditation, in which directed thinking in words and images is used for producing desired mental changes in the meditant, may be considered to be related to that form of self-education which is called 'auto-suggestion'. 'Suggestion' is the name given to the process by which a statement of belief or of a course of action confidently reiterated by another person may create the same belief or course of action in the hearer. An attempt at self-direction by a parallel process of confident repetition to oneself of a formula conveying a belief or course of action is called 'auto-suggestion'. From time to time the practice of auto-suggestion becomes a popular method of inducing desirable personality changes such as giving up smoking or avoiding the mental components of illness. Rather more than forty years ago an auto-suggestion system was popularised by Dr Coué, whose disciples repeated to themselves several times every night and morning the formula: 'Day by day, in every way, I get better and better.'[1] No one carried out the statistical research that would be necessary to discover whether those repeating this formula were in better health than those who did not. Most likely such a research would have discovered no significant difference, although an auto-suggestion with a more specific content such as a statement that the subject would reduce his cigarette smoking might be expected to be more effective. In either case, a limitation of such auto-suggestive techniques of influencing personality and behaviour is

that their effectiveness is likely to be dependent on a general personality characteristic called 'suggestibility'. The highly suggestible
personality is easily receptive of suggestions coming from other
people and may be more easily affected by his own practice of
auto-suggestion; the individual who is resistant to the suggestions of
others may also be resistant to his own auto-suggestions.

Certain religious practices seem to be simply auto-suggestions of
the Coué type. These are the 'acts' recommended in Catholic devotional books in which the reader is told to repeat verbal formulae
embodying attitudes of acceptance of Christian doctrines or of
determination to carry out lines of Christian behaviour. The repetition
of such formulae may have a certain effectiveness with some individuals, but in general, its effectiveness is likely to be limited by the
fact that we are not all equally open to the influence of auto-
suggestion. In the same way, the effectiveness of listening to sermons
as a means of producing desirable character change is limited by the
fact that men are not equally open to the influence of hetero-
suggestion. Such pious 'acts' may, however, be effective in producing
temporary changes of mental set. A Christian worshipper, for
example, may preface his prayer by an act of recollection of the
presence of God, and find that this helps in attaining a prayerful state
of mind.

A more drastic method of producing changes in mental dispositions is the form of mental exercise in which there is prolonged control
of the processes of verbal thinking and mental imagery. There seems
little reason for doubting that such an exercise can produce personality changes if undertaken with energy and determination. Its effects
are likely to be greater than any resulting from the mere recital of
auto-suggestive verbal formulae since it is an activity undertaken
more strenuously and over a longer period of time. Its effectiveness
may also be increased by the use of various mental and physical
preparatory activities.

Different preparatory exercises have been used in different cultures.
They include the use of a verbal formula such as an act of recollection, the adoption of a prescribed bodily posture, and various ways of
controlling the breathing. All of these may contribute to the development of a mental set in which the mind is occupied with one idea and
is free from irrelevant thoughts. This is the condition known in
Eastern meditational practice as 'one-pointedness'. It is not attained
by muscular relaxation which tends rather to favour diffusion of
thought culminating in drowsiness or sleep. The traditional bodily
postures in Hindu meditation are the *asana* positions which are
postures involving some muscular strain. The meditant may, for
example, sit bolt upright with the legs folded so that each foot is
resting on the thigh of the other leg. Yogis are said to remain in such a
position for many hours. It is no doubt more difficult for a Western

man than it is for an Indian to adopt this position but, even for the Indian, it is obviously not a position of relaxation. One may surmise that the point of such postures is that the attention of the meditant is immobilised on to the physical discomfort of the position, and the subsequent fatigue of the attention causes the mind to pass into the condition of one-pointedness in which it can hold a single object of thought in the centre of the mental field.

Although such highly formalised postures have not developed in Christian meditational practice, it is found that both for prayer and meditation the relatively uncomfortable postures of standing or kneeling are better than relaxation on a comfortable chair. While such a relaxed position may help to detach the thoughts from immediate stimuli, it also encourages the uncontrolled wandering of the mind found in reverie or day-dreaming. For this reason it is not favourable for a mental exercise such as meditation in which control of the thoughts plays a principal part.

As an illustration of how strenuous the meditational exercise can be we can take the time-table of the Buddhist Maha Bodhi Centre in Burma as described by Marie Byles.[2] Each day there were four periods of meditation totalling thirteen hours as well as one hour spent in discussion with an instructor. The method used was one of forty practised in Burma. Its central feature was paying attention to the breath coming in and out of the nostrils, considering this as a symbol of impermanence while expressing this impermanence in such words as 'coming-going'. The ultimate aim of Buddhist meditation is the cessation of craving by realisation of the impermanence of all things to which cravings have become attached. Christian meditation may also be concerned with the transitory nature of all earthly things, but it would be inclined to supplement this by an attempt to realise the contrasting permanence of the things belonging to eternity.

Meditation as it has been practised within the Christian tradition has been a somewhat less strenuous mental exercise than the meditation of Buddhism or of the various Yoga systems. Nevertheless it has made considerable demands on the time and energy of those practising it. Thus the *Spiritual exercises* of St Ignatius Loyola were a series of discursive reflections to be made during the course of a retreat lasting for a month.[3] Each meditation took one hour, and five such meditations were carried out each day. Every meditation was preceded by a prayer asking that its performance might be directed to the glory of God. The meditant was then instructed to present to himself the object of his meditation in the form of visual imagery. He then prayed for the appropriate emotion – joy, sorrow, or shame – according to the subject of his meditation. A typical example is the first of the Ignation meditations on three sins. This, like the other meditations, was divided into three parts. The first part dealt with the sin of the fallen angels and the instructions to the meditant were first to carry the memory over this sin, then the understanding, then the will, so that he should blush and be confounded when comparing this one sin of the angels for which they went to hell with the many that he had committed for which he had often deserved hell; then further to apply the *understanding* to this sin of pride by which the angels were changed from grace to malice; and thereupon more to stir the affections by the *will*. In the second and third parts of the meditation he was told to consider in the same manner the sin of Adam and Eve, and the sin of some particular person who has gone to hell. The meditation ended with a colloquy in which the meditant imagined Christ or God the Father or the Blessed Virgin before him and spoke 'just as one friend speaks to another, or a servant to his master, now asking for some favour, now reproaching oneself for some evil done, now telling out one's affairs and seeking counsel in them'.

The effect of the meditation was, no doubt, increased by the circumstance that it was accompanied by solitude, penitence and such exterior penances as fasting. As to attitude, Ignatius instructed his meditants to kneel, to lie prostrate, to lie back with uplifted face, to sit or to stand, whichever seemed appropriate to the aim of the particular stage of the meditation.

After the first week of the Spritual Exercises, Ignatius introduced a somewhat simplified form of meditation which he called a *contemplation*. In this the activity of verbal thinking was reduced to a minimum and more place was given to the activity of visualisation. The topic was generally some incident narrated in the Gospels, such as the presentation of the infant Jesus in the Temple or the raising of Lazarus, and the main activity was the attempt to visualise the scene and incident. The use of the term 'contemplation' for this kind of visual meditation is an awkward one since 'contemplation' is generally used for a form of prayer or a prayer-like state of consciousness in which both verbal thinking and the activity of mental imagery are reduced to a minimum. The kind of meditation in which images rather than words form the main constituents may perhaps be called an 'Ignatian contemplation'.

The Ignatian meditations, like those of the Maha Bodhi centre, had the practical aim of inducing a change in the mental dispositions of the meditants. The object of St Ignatius was to enable the retreatant to make a practical choice between a life in which the religious motive is the dominant one and a more ordinary life in which action is determined by the various impulses which the Buddhists have called 'cravings'. For some of those meditating, this was expected to resolve itself into a choice between the monastic life and life in the world. For all the primary purpose of the meditation was to lead to a choice of what, in Protestant terminology, would be called 'consecration', or self-surrender to the will of God.

Some of the details of the content of the Ignatian meditations would not commend themselves to the modern Christian. Whether or not it is desirable that people should increase their fear of hell by meditating on the topic, it must be recognised that such a method might be a powerful instrument for making changes in the mental dispositions of the persons carrying it out. From the psychological point of view, it would seem to be a method of auto-suggestion carried out under conditions likely to prove favourable to its effectiveness. Those responsible for the use of the meditational methods have regarded them as effective enough in producing mental effects to need the safeguard of a director (or guru) whose experience can guide the changes into desirable channels and help the meditant to avoid undesirable side-effects.

Meditation has played a central part in the spiritual life of those in monastic orders, and is also encouraged amongst devout Catholic laymen. Protestantism, on the other hand, has not much developed the practice of meditation. There may be some loss from this neglect but this loss is not likely to be great since the training of the dispositions aimed at in meditation may also be accomplished by sermons, by scriptural reading and by vocal prayer. In Protestant bodies, listening to sermons fulfils some of the functions of meditation; dispositional training is accomplished by hetero-suggestion in such bodies rather than by auto-suggestion. It seems, however, that meditation may serve a real religious need for which these other activities are not an adequate substitute. This is strongly suggested by the attraction of non-Christian meditational practices for those brought up in a Christian tradition that does not include meditation. The offer of a training in Zen or in some form of Mantra Yoga meets with a ready response in Western countries, implying a need that is not being met by present-day Christian practice. A Christian of today looking for topics on which he felt he ought to train himself to feel more strongly and act more effectively might be less concerned with sin and hell than with poverty and war. But he might find that his emotional drive to effective action on such matters could be strengthened by dis-cursive meditation on Ignatian lines. On the whole, the modern Western man has turned against such methods of controlling his dispositions but this turning away may not be permanent; there is increasing interest in the possibilities of meditation and in future the methods of Ignatius of Loyola may be tried as well as those of Oriental religions.

A Buddhist meditation may also include discursive reflections of somewhat similar character to those in the Ignatian system.[4] The meditant may, for example, be instructed to reflect on his body enveloped by the skin and full of manifest impurity from the top of the head down, thinking of the hair, nails, teeth, sinews, bones, intestines, faeces, bile, etc. with the intention that he should learn to think of himself not as a living person but rather as an aggregate of elements in which he can feel no satisfaction. This would seem to be a method of alteration of mental dispositions of the same kind as that of the Ignatian meditations.

Most meditations so far described have been activities of directed thinking in which verbal processes or trains of imagery were voluntarily produced by the meditant. This fact would have been expressed in early psychological terms as an activity 'of the understanding'. There is, however, another kind of mental exercise in which the object is not a directed process of thinking but a quietness from discursive thinking. Of this kind are the exercises in 'mindfulness' in Buddhism in which attention is paid to the act of breathing or to the physical actions of walking. It is also the characteristic meditational process of Zen Buddhism and of the Hindu Mantra Yoga in which thought is directed on the repetition of a sacred word or formula. Quietness of mind is also found as an aim in the silence of a Quaker meeting or in the act of the presence of God which may precede a Catholic meditation. Where such interior quietness is the aim, the meditation can no longer be regarded as a means of making specific changes in dispositions. The gains are regarded rather as those of increased awareness and widening of consciousness; such gains have been claimed to result also from the use of certain drugs.

The condition of quietness of mind in which directed thinking is reduced to a minimum is also reported to be an end result of habitual discursive meditation on religious topics. St Teresa and other writers on prayer have reported a stage of meditation in which discursive meditation is found to be no longer possible and no voluntary effort to maintain the state is necessary beyond that of keeping the mind from wandering. This condition has been known amongst Catholic writers on prayer as 'the prayer of quiet' which will be further discussed in the chapter on mysticism. It is sharply distinguished by them from the mental state reached by the voluntary suppression of verbal thinking and of mental imagery. This is called 'the prayer of simple regard' or 'acquired contemplation' in contrast to the 'infused contemplation' of the prayer of quiet. The term 'contemplation' is used as a general term for states of consciousness in which the mind remains in imageless concentration on one subject, while 'meditation' is used for the more active process in which directed thinking is employed. A term often used in Eastern religions for the characteristic mental set of contemplation is 'one-pointedness'. This is not well expressed by the familiar psychological term 'concentration' since this implies effort. Perhaps the best psychological equivalent of one-pointedness is 'effortless concentration'.

Although writers on prayer have regarded contemplation as a more advanced stage of spiritual development than meditation it is not, in the Christian tradition, regarded as one that should be directly aimed at. In this respect. Christian practice differs from the systems of spiritual development in Yoga and Buddhism in which mental exercises are prescribed to produce the condition of one-pointedness, such as the repetition of a sacred word or formula in Mantra Yoga. The accepted Christian view that the road to contemplation is through discursive meditation is well expressed by the author of *The cloud of unknowing*:

> whatever man or woman weeneth to come to contemplation without many such sweet meditations beforehand of their own wretchedness, the passion, the kindness, the great goodness and the worthiness of God, surely he shall err and fail of his purpose. And yet, a man or woman that hath long time been practised in these meditations, must nevertheless leave them . . . if ever he shall pierce the cloud of unknowing betwixt him and his God.[5]

When, in the seventeenth century, Molinos seemed to be defending the opposite view, that contemplation should be induced by the deliberate suppression of mental activity in prayer, this teaching was condemned as the heresy of quietism. Thus Molinos said: 'consider nothing, desire nothing, will nothing, endeavour after nothing; and then in everything, thy soul will live reposed with quiet and enjoyment'.[6] Although other passages in Molinos's writings defend the traditional view that the road to contemplation is through discursive meditation, his teaching was strongly opposed by more orthodox theologians, particularly the Jesuits who distrusted the invitation to suspend mental activity as a means to the attainment of contemplation.

There has not been much experimental study by psychologists of the problems of meditation. What there has been is mainly concerned with Eastern forms of meditational practice, particularly with those of Zen Buddhism. A recent example is an investigation by Deikman in which subjects were instructed to concentrate for three periods of five, ten and fifteen minutes respectively on the perception of a blue vase.[7] Although the total time devoted to meditation by these subjects was small, they reported some of the effects on consciousness that are claimed to take place in Zen meditation. Of particular interest is the state referred to as 'deautomisation' in which the object is seen as if for the first time without the dulling effect of the habituation which has resulted from previous perceptual experience of the same kind. This is related to the religious experience described by William James and others in which all things are seen as new but it is described here without any religious reference. Deautomisation is an experience which is potentially religious; it was also reported by Aldous Huxley as one of the effects of taking mescalin.[8]

There have also been studies of Zen meditations by the use of recordings of electric currents from the brain.[9] These confirm that the state of consciousness achieved by Zen meditation is also a neuro-physiological reality with appearance òf the alpha-rhythm characteristic of relaxed wakefulness. In Zen meditation, however, this shows increase in amplitude and decrease of frequency succeeded in many cases by the appearance of a theta-rhythm. These characteristics indicate a trance-like state but one different from the hypnotic trance. These changes in brain current are found to be correlated with the proficiency of the subject in his Zen training. An interesting point is that during a meditation of a Zen master there was no habituation to a click stimulus as found in normal people. This is consistent with the appearance of deautomisation (or the perceptual world appearing new) which is a reported conscious concomitant of Zen meditation.

These investigations are, of course, only scratching at the surface of the experimental problems of meditation. There seems to be no corresponding study of the neuro-physiological side of meditation as carried out within the Christian tradition. We have no assured knowledge on the much more difficult question of the effects of meditation in their permanent influence on behaviour and on spiritual growth. There have been some attempts to explore meditational techniques as an aid to psychotherapy but much more remains to be found out about the lasting effects of meditation on the development of the personality.[10]

## REFERENCES

1. C. H. Brooks, *The practice of autosuggestion by the method of Emile Coué*, London, 1922.
2. Marie B. Byles, *Journey into Burmese silence*, London, 1962.
3. W. H. Longridge, *The spiritual exercises of Saint Ignatius of Loyola*, London, 1919.
4. Buddhist Publication Society, *The foundations of mindfulness* (Satipaṭṭhāna Sutta), Kandy.
5. Anonymous, *The cloud of unknowing* (reprinted), London, 1924.
6. M. de Molinos, *The spiritual guide* (Eng. trans.), London, 1699.
7. A. J. Deikman, 'Experimental meditation' in *Altered states of consciousness* (Ed. C. T. Tart), New York and London, 1969.
8. A. Huxley, *The doors of perception*, London, 1954.
9. Akira Kasamatsu and Tomio Hirai, 'An electroencephalographic study on the Zen meditation (zazen)' in *Altered states of consciousness* (Ed. C. T. Tart), London and New York, 1969.
10. W. Kretschmer, 'Meditative techniques in psychotherapy' in *Altered states of consciousness* (Ed. C. T. Tart), London and New York, 1969.

# 14. The psychology of conversion

'Religious conversion' is the name commonly given to the process which leads to the adoption of a religious attitude; the process may be gradual or sudden. It is likely to include a change in belief on religious topics but this will be accompanied by changes in the motivation to behaviour and in reactions to the social environment. One or other of these directions of change may seem to play the predominant role in the conversion change; one may then speak of *intellectual*, of *moral*, or of *social* conversions. The distinctions between them are not, however, clear cut; every intellectual change has its implications for behaviour and for social allegiances, and no one is likely to change his social allegiance in religion or his behaviour motivation without some corresponding change in what he believes.

We may take as a typical account of a sudden conversion that of St Paul, described in Acts 9. It will be remembered that Saul, an orthodox and zealous Jew, was active in persecution of the Christians. He went from Jerusalem towards Damascus with authority from the high priest to arrest the Christians there. On his way, he had a vision of light and an auditory experience of a voice, ostensibly that of Jesus Christ, reproaching him for his persecutions and directing him to go to Damascus where he would be told what to do. He then found himself blind until a few days later a man called Ananias laid his hands on him telling him that he would recover his sight and be filled with the Holy Ghost. Then Saul recovered his sight, and after baptism, started preaching in the synagogues that Jesus was the son of God.

The story has interested psychologists particularly in its suddenness and in the intensified hostility to Christianity immediately preceding it. The visual experience of light at the moment of conversion is a not uncommon feature, although I know of no plausible psychological explanation. The psychogenic blindness relieved only at the moment of final surrender has also been considered to be of psychological interest although it is an unusual feature of conversion stories. The character of increased hostility to the finally accepted attitude has a psychological explanation if we assume that the final acceptance has already taken place at some level before the individual has become aware of it. There are mental processes that actively resist changes of belief. Such are the processes of 'rationalisation' which may provide reasons for continuing to hold a belief system after it has been undermined by contrary evidence or by the development of a new attitude. The affective bias towards maintaining an old system of thought may be strong; the holder may be unwilling to give up the comforts of certain conviction and to pass through the unpleasant and insecure condition of doubt. He may also be unwilling to give up the comfort and security he received from his membership of the social group to which he belonged by virtue of his old opinion. So it is understandable that his first reaction to a threat to an established belief system may be to produce new rationalisations in its support, and to show the behaviour pattern of increased intolerance towards those who threaten his old belief. As the forces acting against the cherished belief system accumulate, however, the system may suddenly collapse and the arguments previously used in its support may be seen to be mere rationalisations. A similar process may occur in a non-religious setting, resulting in a change of mind to which we are inclined to apply the same name. The above is a psychological account of what takes place in a religious conversion and may be correct but this does not imply that it is complete; it may well be that more can be said about the process of religious conversion from a theological point of view.

The idea that the psychological process in such a religious change as a sudden conversion might be one in which changes in attitude were taking place slowly but outside the limits of consciousness was called by William James the theory of 'subconscious incubation'.[1] The type of psychological thinking that has developed from Freud's system of psycho-analysis has given these ideas greater plausibility and precision. Instead of regarding subconsciousness or unawareness as a more or less accidental property of some kinds of mental processes, this system of thought considers that there is an active process of *repression* by which that which is painful or incompatible with the purposes of the main stream of consciousness is banished into a region called the *unconscious* from which it may influence behaviour or conscious processes of thought but cannot be voluntarily made a part of the conscious stream of thought.

Of the three classes of religious conversion already distinguished (intellectual, moral and social) St Paul's conversion would seem to belong to the third class. The primary change seems to have been from one system of loyalties to another; there is no evidence that the conflict was one between opposing opinions, still less that it was a conflict between a righteous and an unrighteous system of moral motivation: St Paul seems to have been a rigidly righteous man before and after his conversion. In contrast with this there is the type of conversion change more usually described by revival preachers in which the convert gives up a sinful way of life and accepts the way of righteousness. As an example we may take the case of 'Swearing Tom', converted after a sermon preached in a small church at Basingstoke.[2]

'Swearing Tom' had earned his nickname by ungodliness and profane language. He was reported to have been a leader in sin and profanity, and had not, for seventeen years, entered a church. It was said that only curiosity brought him to church on this occasion. The preacher took as his text the words 'I will put a new spirit within you'. At the end of his address, he said: 'If the most wicked man in this church would go home and pray that God, for Christ's sake, would give him His Holy Spirit to change his heart, God would hear and answer that man's prayer.'

These words, we are told, went straight to the heart of 'Swearing Tom'. 'I am the worst man here,' he said to himself; 'I will go home and pray.' Passing by the familiar public-house, he refused to turn in. On reaching home he threw himself on his knees, and tried to pray in the words which he had heard from the pulpit. The prayer was answered. From that time he became a changed man, and his name of 'Swearing Tom' was soon altered to that of 'Praying Tom' by which he was known until the day of his death.

Here the conflict seems to have been primarily a moral one, and the change to be essentially the adopting of a new way of life, although other psychological factors may also have entered into the conversion which are not mentioned here. Such anecdotal material must certainly be approached with caution; it should be treated rather as illustrative material than as a sound basis for psychological conclusions. Particularly where, as in this case, it has been written for the purpose of edification, there may be unintended falsification in the narrative. In memory there may be much smoothing of the record to make it conform to the conventional pattern of what the recorder thinks ought to have happened while jarring elements are left out. There is certainly conventionalisation of the actual experience – those belonging to a religious group tend to go through the experiences characteristic of that group – and there is probably even more conventionalisation of the conversion narratives. There may also be incompleteness in the records themselves since some of the factors in the conversion may be unconscious. We may, for example, feel some doubt as to 'Swearing Tom's' statement that he was drawn to church merely by curiosity. It may have seemed so to him, but it could have been the effect on behaviour of a subconsciously incubating religious attitude; he may, as has been suggested in the case of St Paul, already have accepted the Christian religion subconsciously before he entered the church.

It is less easy to find examples of conversion of the predominantly intellectual type where the essential conflict is between two systems of thought and the decision is that the new one is true and the previously held one is false. Such intellectual conversions may, of course, be either to or from a religious system of thought. They are perhaps commoner in literature than in real life. Mrs Ward's novel *Robert Elsmere* is a good literary example of the description of a purely intellectual conversion, from Christianity to agnosticism, as Masefield's *The everlasting mercy* is of a moral conversion to Christianity. Both are interesting examples of what is meant by these terms; both are fictitious and cannot therefore be used as a basis for drawing conclusions.

A purely intellectual conversion, uncomplicated by elements of moral or social conflict, is perhaps not to be found in real life. Certainly one will not find them in the records of evangelists since these do not commonly argue with individual members of their audiences and generally doubt the value of an intellectual appeal. Yet there are cases of individuals whose main problem has been that of accepting as true the propositions of religion and whose central change has been the acceptance of a system of beliefs that was previously held to be false. No doubt, other factors come into such a person's conversion; he must change his behaviour motivation and his loyalties too, but the change of belief may seem to him to be the primary thing from which these others follow.

A recent example of such a predominantly intellectual conversion is that of Professor Joad; a more ancient one very fully recorded is that of St Augustine. Joad was a professor of philosophy whose training constrained him to accept what seemed to him the most rational view of the world. He records that until comparatively late in his life the deliverances of reason no less than the weight of the evidence seemed to him to tell heavily against the religious view of the universe. Without ceasing to feel that, as a matter of psychological compulsion, he must adopt the most rational hypothesis, he tells how he gradually came to believe that the most rational hypothesis was the religious view of the world, both the general religious view of two orders of reality, a natural and a supernatural, and also the specifically Christian view which includes the belief that Jesus Christ was in part a supernatural as well as in part a natural person.[3] While Joad recounts little of the non-intellectual elements in the conflict leading to his conversion, he does indicate that it had implications in the field of moral valutations. He describes how he lost his agreeable immunity from the sense of sin. 'My eyes', he said, 'were gradually opened to the extent of my own sinfulness in thought, word and deed . . . I came whole-heartedly to endorse the account of me given in the English *Book of Common Prayer*.'

St Augustine (of Hippo) experienced a conversion of a mixed type in which the moral conflict loomed large but the intellectual factor played a predominant part, as would be expected in another teacher of philosophy. He describes in the seventh book of the *Confessions* his intellectual difficulties in the acceptance of Christianity.[4] In particular, he found himself unable to understand the cause of evil. He knew that evil was supposed to be the result of human free-will, but this consideration did not seem to him to supply a solution to his difficulties. 'For', said St Augustine, 'he (God) would not be omnipotent if he could not create any good things unless he were supplied with matter which he himself did not create. These things did I toss up and down in this miserable heart of mine, which was made heavy through most biting cares, through the fear of death and of not finding out the truth.' By a study of Scripture, he came to have what he considered to be a right view of all these questions, and he accepted the view that iniquity was the perversion of the will. Yet, although he accepted Jesus Christ as the mediator between God and man, he failed to understand what he afterwards regarded as the true doctrine of the Incarnation, not grasping the implications of the teaching that 'The Word was made flesh.' These difficulties disappeared when he studied the writings of St Paul.

He now accepted the Catholic faith, but, although his intellectual conflict was resolved, his conversion was not complete; there was still a moral conflict to be resolved. Earlier in the *Confessions,* he tells how 'the custom of satisfying an insatiable desire of lust did chiefly and vehemently torment me'. Arrangements were made for him to be legally married so that he might be baptised. In preparation for this marriage, he was separated from the mistress who was his bed-fellow, and he reports 'my heart that cleaved to her was broken and wounded until it bled ... To thee be praise, to thee be glory, O thou fountain of mercies. I grew the more miserable, and thou camest nearer to me'.

With his intellectual conflict resolved, this moral conflict still remained, opposing a resistance to the process of conversion. 'Thus sick in mind and tormented was I, accusing myself bitterly beyond all custom, and turning and winding myself in my chain, until such time as it might be wholly broken; for though but little, it yet held me.' Torn between the attractions of his old mistresses and of 'the chaste dignity of Continence', he wept in the most bitter sorrow of his heart.

While still weeping, he heard a child chanting the words: 'Take up and read.' He took this as a command from God, and opened a Bible at random. His eyes fell on the passage: 'Not in rioting and drunkenness, not in chambering and wantonness, not in strife and envying; but put ye on the Lord Christ and make no provision for the flesh and its concupiscences.' 'No further would I read', said St Augustine, 'nor was there cause why I should; for instantly with the end of this sentence, as by a clear and constant light infused into my heart, the darkness of all former doubts was driven away.' The conversion process was now complete.

This is one of the great conversion stories of the world. Its narrator had a remarkable power of describing his own states of mind, and shows insight into the moral conflict which accompanied his intellectual conflict. Clearly these two conflicts interacted; it seems reasonable to suppose that St Augustine's intellectual difficulties about sin were in part a reflection of the conflict between his own moral ideals and his actual behaviour. Yet there seems no reason for supposing that his intellectual conflict was merely a rationalisation of his moral conflict. He was a teacher of philosophy, so his choice of belief system would depend even more than other people's on purely logical considerations about the apparent truth of a belief system, and not merely on his emotional and behavioural needs. His conversion was in large part a change of intellectual conviction.

The third type of conversion experience distinguished above was called the *social conversion* in which the main conflict seems to be that between loyalties to opposing groups. In our own community where there is no strong social bond between members of the same religious group, the social conflict in a religious change is not likely to be severe. A modern Englishman may become a Theosophist, a Muslim or an atheist without making much difference to his circle of friends and without tearing apart any of the bonds that bind him to his family. But in other times, and at the present time in other communities, this may not be true. A change of religious affiliation may entail a breach with all the people with whom one has had intimate social relationships, even with members of one's own family. Such was the case in the social situation in which St Paul was converted to Christianity; the conflict was with a system of social loyalties which must be broken if the new religion were accepted.

A more recent example of a conversion of the social type is that of the Sadhu Sundar Singh who was converted from Hinduism to Christianity. The following is an account of his conversion in his own words:

When I was out in any town I got people to throw stones at Christian preachers. I would tear up the Bible and burn it when I had a chance. In the presence of my father I cut up the Bible and other Christian books and put kerosene oil upon them and burnt them. I thought this was a false religion and tried all I could to destroy it. I was faithful to my own religion, but I could not get any satisfaction or peace, though I performed all the ceremonies and rites of that religion. So I thought of leaving it all and committing suicide. Three days after I had burnt the Bible, I woke up about three o'clock in the morning, had my usual bath and prayed, 'O God, if there is a God, wilt thou show me the right way or I will kill myself.' My intention was that, if I got no satisfaction, I would place my head upon the railway line when the 5 o'clock train passed by and kill myself. If I got no satisfaction in this life, I thought I would get it in the next. I was praying and praying but got no answer; and I prayed for half-an-hour longer hoping to get

peace. At 4.30 a.m. I saw something of which I had no idea at all
previously. In the room where I was praying I saw a great light. I
thought the place was on fire. I looked round, but could find
nothing. Then the thought came to me, 'Jesus Christ is not dead but
living and it must be He Himself.' So I fell at His feet and got this
wonderful Peace which I could not get anywhere else. This is the
joy I was wishing to get. This was heaven itself. When I got up, the
vision had all disappeared; but although the vision disappeared the
Peace and Joy have remained with me ever since. I went off and
told my father that I had become a Christian.[5]

As in the case of St Paul, this account suggests a period of
subconscious incubation. The Sadhu's mounting hostility to Christianity in the period before his conversion suggests that Christianity
may already have been accepted unconsciously, while his affection for
his parents and other social bonds tying him to his old religious
loyalties formed a resistance against the emergence of his Christian
convictions into consciousness. The suddenness of the conversion
seems better explained as the sudden breaking down of the resistance
to an already existing conviction than as the sudden appearance of a
new one.

In view of the psychological interest of the conversion process, it is
not surprising to find that one of the earliest psychological studies of a
religious phenomenon by the use of a scientific method of enquiry was
a study of conversion. This is plainly a field in which strictly
experimental methods cannot be used but Starbuck, at the close of the
nineteenth century, started to study it by what were then somewhat
novel methods, sending out to a number of people a typed set of
questions and then classifying their answers and subjecting them to a
process of numerical analysis.[6] To William James, this did not seem
to be a promising way of approaching the problems of religion and he
has recorded in his preface to Starbuck's book how he tried to
discourage him from his project. He also records, however, that he
was convinced that he had been wrong in condemning Starbuck's
proposed methods of study which had justified themselves by their
results.

Starbuck was particularly concerned with the commonest age for
conversion. His figures confirmed the general impression that conversion is above all an adolescent phenomenon. He analysed a
number of reports of conversion experiences and condensed these into
a typical experience which had three successive phases: dejection and
sadness, a point of transition, and lastly, joy and peace. He made a
comparative study of conversions that occurred in regular church
activities and those that resulted from the activity of a professional
evangelist. He found that more conversions occurred under the latter
conditions but that a very much larger number of these lapsed within

a period of six weeks, and that those who remained within the church congregation were predominantly those converted during the regular work of the church. Starbuck also made a numerical comparison of those who experienced sudden conversion with those who showed a more gradual spiritual growth without a conversion crisis. While there were differences in the religious lives of these groups, Starbuck's general finding was that the religious development of the two groups was, on the whole, remarkably parallel.

Although James paid tribute to the success of Starbuck's attempt to apply empirical methods to the study of religion, it must be admitted that Starbuck's use of these methods falls short of the standards that would be applied to such a study at the present day. Starbuck seems not to have considered sufficiently how far the response to a system of questions may be determined by the form of the questions asked; a critic might reasonably object that the investigator started with a clear picture of what a conversion experience was and asked his subjects how well their experiences conformed to that picture. In addition, he seems to have been insufficiently careful to ensure that his subjects were a representative sample of the population as a whole. Later studies of the use of questionnaire methods have shown how important is the use of an unbiassed sample. Also he asserted differences when these may have been merely accidental differences in the figures obtained; he was working before modern methods of determining the significance of numerical differences had been developed. These defects do not detract from the merits of Starbuck as a pioneer in the application of empirical methods to the psychological study of religion; they are grounds for not regarding his detailed results as of lasting value. They do, however, raise questions which later workers may answer by the use of more adequate methods.

It can hardly be questioned that Starbuck was right in his emphasis on adolescence as the typical period for the occurrence of religious conversion. This does not, however, imply that we should accept the formula adopted by some writers on religion who say that conversion is a phenomenon of adolescence. Rather it seems to be the case that there is one kind of conversion with certain well-marked distinctive characteristics which takes place only during the period of adolescence and seems to be by far the most frequently encountered. An example of an adolescent conversion is that of William Booth, founder of the Salvation Army, as told by Harold Begbie.[7]

Of the days before his conversion, General Booth said: 'I have often wondered that I did not go straight to hell.' It seems, however, that he was condemning himself for nothing worse than having been a high-spirited leader in the village games while he was indifferent to higher things. There was no religious atmosphere in his home and attendance at his parish church as a child made no particular impression on him. He was, however, impressed by the separate and religious life of one of his cousins, and records having at one time been much affected by the hymn 'Here we suffer grief and pain'. These impressions faded and he settled down to an indifference with which he felt an inward dissatisfaction.

At this time his family was plunged into poverty. Instead of becoming a gentleman, William Booth went into a pawnbroker's shop at the age of thirteen, which caused him lasting shame. From this time, he began to be interested in religion and to attend chapel. He began to feel that the religious life was superior to the purely worldly existence he had lived for fourteen years, and a hunger sprang up for it. 'I wanted', he said, 'to be right with God. I wanted to be right in myself. I wanted a life spent in putting other people right.' While this unhappiness was increasing and also his sense of the reality of God, he devoted himself with zeal to the interests of his employer; he meant to get on in the world. At the same time he became interested in political reform. He was deeply affected by the miseries of the people around him, and his sympathy with the poor was shown by his adherence to the Chartists. During the year of his conversion, he saw children crying for bread in the streets of Nottingham.

In his sixteenth year, he determined to make the 'surrender of personality' which precedes conversion, but he was held back by the memory of a sin. In a boyish trading affair, he had made a profit out of his companions, but they, not knowing this, had been grateful to him and had given him a silver pencil-case as a token of gratitude. He found it difficult to admit the deception but resolved to do so, and he acknòwledged what he had done to the person chiefly wronged, and returned the pencil-case. Now he felt that the guilty burden had rolled away from his heart, and that peace had come in its place. This was the moment of his conversion; he was happy.

He reported that he then felt that he could willingly and joyfully travel to the ends of the earth for Jesus Christ, and suffer anything imaginable to help the souls of other men. He says:

> Rather than yearning for the world's pleasures, books, gains, or recreations, I found my nature leading me to come away from it all. It had lost all charm for me. What were all the novels, even those of Sir Walter Scott or Fenimore Cooper, compared with the story of my Saviour? What were the choicest orators compared with Paul? What was the hope of my money-earning, even with all my desire to help my poor mother and sisters, in comparison with the imperishable wealth of ingathered souls? I soon began to despise everything that the world had to offer me.

Nevertheless, it is reported that he continued to be the cleverest and most dependable of his employer's staff. One may reasonably suspect that the reference to despising everything that the world had to offer him somewhat exaggerated the degree of renunciation in the attitude of the boy at that time. His wonder that he had not gone straight to hell earlier is an expression of self-condemnation that may also be suspected of containing a considerable element of exaggeration. Exaggeration of pre-conversion sinfulness and of post-conversion virtue are characteristics of adolescent conversion. One can find numerous examples of these tendencies in Starbuck's records. A male convert of sixteen, for example, is reported to have said of his state before conversion: 'my mind was in a state of great anxiety. The fleshly mind was all aflame, and my guilt was hideous to me. Because I belonged to church I felt myself a hypocrite'.

The opposite tendency is illustrated by a female convert who said of her state after conversion: 'I was a new creature in Christ Jesus. Everything seemed heavenly rather than earthly: everything was so lovely. I had a love for everybody. It was such a blessed experience. Going home I walked on the curbstone rather than walk or talk with ungodly people.'

No doubt, when conversion stories are told for the purpose of edification, part of this exaggeration is to make the stories more edifying. The abandonment of sin, for example, is the more improving to an audience as the depth of the sin was greater. But there is probably more than this in the tendency. Pre-conversion sin may be described in terms more suitable for a hardened criminal than for an erring child because part of the emotional experience of his conversion is that his previous life appears so to him. Similarly there may be a real experience behind the exaggeration of post-conversion virtue and the appearance of exaggeration may arise from the inevitable difference between the point of view of the convert himself and that of other people around him. The convert judges himself subjectively by the rich emotional experiences of his new life. Other people judge him from observation of his behaviour and this may seem to them in many cases not to be strikingly better than it was before. The convert may be impressed by her new feeling of love for everybody; her neighbours may observe only the behaviour reaction of walking on the curbstone in order to avoid contact with ungodly people.

Another striking feature of adolescent conversions that comes out strongly in reading Starbuck's collection of narratives is their tendency to follow a well-defined course. One notices too a much greater dependence than in adult conversions on personal influence, such as that of a preacher, as well as a marked tendency to impermanence. These characteristics suggest that they are largely a product of suggestion rather than a result of development in the convert's own spiritual life.

There is, however, another possible explanation of the conventional character of adolescent conversions. Not only may they follow a convention developed in the religious tradition in which they occur, but they may also resemble one another in being products of the same developmental fact. All psychological writers have agreed that the essential developmental fact underlying adolescent conversion is the system of conflicts which result from the emergence into consciousness of the impulses connected with the sex instinct.

Some writers have regarded adolescent conversion as merely the normal psychic change at adolescence which has been given a religious colouring. Starbuck has pointed out truly that one of the features of the beginning of the sex life is the arousal of altruistic sentiments, and he appears to regard the sense of sin which accompanies conversion as revulsion from the previous egocentric life.

This does not, however, seem to be borne out by what his adolescent converts themselves say. 'The fleshly mind was all aflame' does not describe a reaction against egocentricity. It suggests rather a reaction against sexual feeling. Starbuck's adolescent converts must be regarded as products of the attitude towards sexuality of their time, in which sexual feeling tended to be regarded as intrinsically sinful and its appearance in one's own consciousness was productive of feelings of guilt. The typical adolescent conversion may be regarded psychologically as the sudden emergence into consciousness of a previously repressed system of feelings belonging to the sex instinct, which is now admitted into consciousness because it is sublimated, purified and directed to a religious end.

In support of this view of the nature of these adolescent conversions, it must be noticed that when adolescents of that period spoke of sin and temptation to sin, they nearly always meant sexual behaviour or sexual thoughts. They were not concerned about the sins and imperfections that an older person might reproach himself for: lovelessness, self-centredness, or indifference to the sufferings of others. This predominant interest in sex as the root of all imperfections is the result, no doubt, in part of the fact that the problem of how to adjust himself to the demands of the sex-life is necessarily a central problem of adolescent behaviour, just as the central behaviour problem of a much older man must be that of adjusting himself to the fact of approaching death. It is also, however, no doubt the product of a particular kind of education about sex: the adolescent had been taught to feel guilty about sex. Under the influence of Freud and modern educators we no longer believe it is right to attach guilt feelings to sex itself but only to particular forms of sex behaviour. If modern education makes the adolescent feel relatively neutral about the fact of sex, this may well affect the form of adolescent conversion experiences. It may still be true that conversions will take place predominantly at adolescence, for adolescence will remain a time of stress however much attitudes may change towards the emerging sexual impulses. But their form may very well be changing as a result of the changing attitudes of adolescents towards their problems. It may be, for example, that diffused guilt feelings would be less common in adolescent conversions at the present day than they were in the time of Starbuck. A more modern research investigation of adolescent conversion along Starbuck's lines would tell us how far these expected changes in the character of adolescent religious conversion are in fact taking place.

Although there is no doubt that the majority of conversions take place at or about the period of adolescence, one cannot unreservedly accept the formula 'conversion is a phenomenon of adolescence' since it is also a fact that many of the conversions that have been of most importance in religious history are exceptions to this rule. A large number of great religious leaders have been converted late in life; St Paul, St Augustine, Pascal and Tolstoy are outstanding examples. There are considerable psychological differences between these conversions and the typical adolescent conversion; it seems better, therefore, to treat them as belonging to a different category from that of the ordinary conversion at adolescence. Many of those experiencing this non-adolescent type of conversion have recorded an earlier conversion experience which took the typical adolescent form; in other cases the converted individual is reported to have been very religious from childhood. Thus Pascal was first converted at the age of twenty-three and his second conversion took place eight years later. Evan Roberts, the leader of the Welsh revival at the beginning of this century, was religious from his boyhood and devoted to prayer and Bible-reading. He was converted with soul anguish in 1904, and after that time he had paroxysms and saw visions. Al Ghazzali, who was a professor of Islamic theology at Baghdad, describes how he passed from dogmatic religion through a period of scepticism until he was redeemed by a light which God caused to penetrate into his heart, and afterwards he gave up his professorship and became a *sufi* (a Muslim mystic).[8]

The most striking difference between these later conversions and the typical adolescent conversion is that they are not changes from a non-religious to a religious attitude but from a merely conventional acceptance of the socially approved pattern of religious life to an attitude in which the religious motive becomes dominant and in which religious belief and behaviour become more personal and even possibly idiosyncratic. Thus John Wesley lived as a devout Christian for more than a dozen years after his first conversion, and then underwent a second conversion experience at the age of thirty-five which led to the intense preaching activity of fifty years during which he travelled widely throughout the country and preached 40,000 sermons. Some of Wesley's biographers, in view of the fact that he was a Christian before, have been inclined to doubt the reality of this second conversion. It is, however, only one of many examples of a mature conversion generically different from an adolescent conversion, in which the change is from an ordinary religious life to an attitude in which religious motivation becomes dominant.

While in some cases of mature conversions, such as Wesley's, the re-direction is towards intensified external activity, there are also mature conversions which are turnings from a conventional religious attitude to the more interior religious life of the mystic. This class of mature religious conversions may be called that of 'mystical conversions'. The religious conversions of Al Ghazzali and Pascal were of this type. Typically, the subject of a mystical conversion is a conventionally religious person who lives the usual life of a devout person and may be much respected for his piety and good works. He himself is not satisfied and yearns for something more than his religious life is giving him. He may begin to cut himself adrift from his accustomed life. Then, after a period of unhappiness due to painful inner conflict, he passes through an experience which he may be unable to describe, but which contains a revelation in the light of which his subsequent life must be lived. He may become more or less cut off from his previous social environment and increasingly absorbed in an interior life unintelligible to other people. He may join a contemplative religious order whose members will understand and perhaps share his experiences, but, if he remains in the world, he may find that he is no longer respected. He may, at any rate in the early stages of his new life, find that he experiences such abnormal phenomena as visions and trances, which create scandal amongst those who previously thought well of him.

A story of mystical conversion following closely on these lines is that of Rulman Merswin.[9] He was a wealthy, pious, and respected merchant of Strasbourg. At the age of thirty-six, he retired from business to devote himself to religious matters. One evening in the following autumn as he was strolling in his garden and meditating, a picture of the crucifix suddenly presented itself to his mind. Merswin was filled with a violent hatred of the world and of his own free-will. 'Lifting his eyes to heaven, he solemnly swore that he would utterly surrender his own will, person, and goods to the service of God'. This act of surrender was at once followed by the vision of a brilliant light, the hearing of a divine voice of adorable sweetness and a feeling as if he were lifted from the ground. When he came to himself, his heart was filled by a new consciousness of the divine and by a transport of intense love towards God which drove him to acts of mortification. From this incident of conversion, he dated the beginning of his real life.

We have only fragmentary knowledge of what appears to have been a similar mystical conversion experienced by St Thomas Aquinas in 1273. He had led an actively intellectual religious life of which the best known fruit is his great *Summa Theologiae*. Then at the age of forty-eight, he had an experience which inhibited further literary composition. 'I can write no more', he said, 'for everything that I have written seems like straw, by comparison with the things which I have now seen. and which have been revealed to me.'[10]

Much more fully documented is the mystical conversion of Pascal about four centuries later. He was typical in that he was devout before his mystical conversion. Before he was twenty-four, he is reported to have been enlightened by God through the reading of books of piety so that he 'understood perfectly that the Christian religion obliges us to live only for God and to have no other object than Him'. He had always been orthodox in religion and virtuous in life. Two further factors that affected his religious life were the influence of the puritanically inclined Jansenists and a chronic invalidism which limited his intellectual activity. He seems also to have been in love with a woman of rank whom he could not hope to marry.

But he felt dissatisfied with the things of the world and under the influence of his sister who was a nun, he decided at the age of thirty 'to leave altogether all the intercourse of the world, and to cut off all the superfluities of life, even at the peril of his health'. But the change was not yet complete. He had learned to despise the world but not to love God. His own efforts to redirect his will proved ineffective. In November 1654, he heard a sermon in which the preacher insisted upon the necessity for entire surrender to God. Shortly after this, Pascal fell into a trance in which he had a vivid impression of the presence of God, and seemed to be illuminated by a supernatural fire. This was his mystical conversion which initiated a new life of obedience and submission to the will of God. The record of this conversion experience was found. after his death on a paper worn over his heart:

> The year of grace 1654. Monday November the 23rd ... From about half past ten in the evening to about half past midnight. Fire.
>
> God of Abraham. God of Isaac. God of Jacob. Not of the philosophers and of the learned. Certainty. Certainty. Feeling. Joy. Peace. God of Jesus Christ. Deum meum et Deum vestrum. Thy God shall be my God - Forgetful of the world and of all except God. One finds him only by the ways taught in the Gospel. Greatness of the human soul. Righteous Father, the world has not known thee, but I have known thee. Joy, joy. joy, tears of joy ... My God will you leave me? May I not be separated from him eternally.
>
> This is eternal life, knowing thee the only true God and the one sent by you J.-C. Jesus Christ. Jesus Christ. I have been separated from him: I have fled from him. renounced him. crucified him. May I never be separated from him.[11]

In these moving but somewhat incoherent words. Pascal reminded himself of the experience which changed his life and started him on the road of mystical development.

These accounts of mystical conversion show some common psychological features. In the preliminary conflict that leads to the conversion, the subject is not merely avoiding sin but is also denying himself the satisfaction of his own elementary instinctive desires for food, comfort and companionship. He may even be denying himself a satisfaction valued generally even by the devout, the good opinion of his fellow men. He is trying to rid himself of all those desires (or cravings) that bind him to this world in order that he may direct his energies towards spiritual ends. If we use the term 'libido' for the general energy behind such particular desires as hunger, love, and self-assertion, we may say that the subject of a mystical conversion is trying to divert his libido from the external world in order that he may direct it to the spiritual world, or, as the theistic mystic would say, to God. To accomplish this, he does violence to his natural affections. He may try to get rid of his addiction to bodily comfort by scourging himself or fasting; he may do violence to his self-regarding sentiment by allowing his body to become disfigured by neglect and by other actions which will provoke the contempt of other people; he may shut himself away from his fellow men so that he does not obtain satisfaction from his gregarious tendencies.

Since love for a particular human being makes greater demands on the libido than any other sentiment, it is the one that the person engaged in the conflict preceding the mystical conversion most sternly avoids. It is likely that the failure to find a satisfactory resting-place for his libido in a human love object may often be the determining incident which turned his feet into the path which led to mystical conversion. Pascal has recorded his own failure to find happiness in love in his *Discourse on the passions of love*. St Catherine of Genoa and Mme Guyon are examples of great unhappiness in married life before their mystical conversions. It would, of course, be incorrect to say that the person undergoing mystical conversion has turned his back on human love. He has turned his back on love for a particular human object; there may also be an initial breaking of the emotional bonds with other people. But while the abandonment of particular love is lasting, the cutting off from other people is a transitory phase. In the later stages of the mystical life, there is a strong development of love for all others. In this respect the Christian mystic does not differ from the Buddhist arahat; he, too, has destroyed cravings, but has developed compassionate love for all living creatures.

There is, however, something in this initial turning away from human affections which may make the record of a mystical conversion somewhat repellent to readers who are otherwise sympathetic to religion and even to religious mysticism. The convert of the ordinary type may abandon drink or drugs and turn to a respectable way of living; with his conversion all can sympathise. But when we hear of the mystical convert not merely treating his body with

unreasonable severity but also abandoning the ties of human affection, even perhaps ceasing to live a socially useful life, we may feel
that this is something with which no reasonable person can
sympathise. Yet the inner necessity which drives the mystical convert
to these excesses seems to him to be a driving force which he would be
wrong to resist; Suso and other mystics have felt the impulse to lead
an ordinary, decent, and respectable Christian life as a subtle and
dangerous temptation. They feel that they have to forego all pleasure-
giving activities even of the most harmless or commendable kind, if
they are to avoid failing to attain their goal. This initial turning away
from social entanglements even of a morally harmless kind is not
confined to those individuals who undergo mystical conversion; it is
found also in other people who have diverted their libido to some
other end. A devoted scientific research worker may show the same
tendency to indifference to the demands of natural affection. The
mystical convert's reaction to the temptation to lead an ordinary
useful and respectable religious life may be paralleled by a research
worker's temptation to leave the investigations which engross him in
order to do work which is also socially valuable but which is
sufficiently remunerative to enable him to marry and live in comfort.
He too may feel that if he were to yield to this temptation he would be
selling his soul. Other people may condemn his single-minded devotion to his chosen path no less than they do that of the subject of
mystical conversion.

Whether such restrictions on behaviour are regarded as sacrifices
for a worth-while end or merely as unhealthy quirks of personality
development depends on one's evaluation of the end to which they are
directed. In the case of mystical conversion, this end is the contemplative life. This is an end which is generally less valued at the
present day than are the advancement of knowledge and the improvement in technology that are the aims of scientific research. The
psychologist may reasonably feel that he is not called upon to
pronounce judgment on the value of religious contemplation as an
end. He should, however, realise that different evaluations of the
contemplative life are possible. To those concerned only with this
world, mysticism may appear merely a diversion of human energies
into unfruitful channels. There is, however, also the view expressed by
Aldous Huxley that 'the end of human life is contemplation, or the
direct and intuitive awareness of God ... the existence of at least a
minority of contemplatives is necessary for the well-being of any
society'.[12]

## REFERENCES

1. W. James, *The varieties of religious experience,* London, 1902.
2. C. S. Isaacson. *Stories of grace,* London, 1905.
3. C. E. M. Joad. *The recovery of belief: a restatement of Christian philosophy,* London. 1952.
4. Saint Augustine. *The confessions of St Augustine* (Eng. trans.), London. 1923.
5. B. H. Streeter and A. J. Appasamy, *The Sadhu,* London, 1921.
6. E. D. Starbuck. *The psychology of religion,* London. 1899.
7. H. Begbie. *Life of W. Booth,* London. 1920.
8. C. Field. *The confessions of Al Ghazzali,* London. 1909.
9. Evelyn Underhill. *Mysticism,* London. 1911.
10. V. White. *God and the unconscious,* London. 1952.
11. P. Faugere. *Pensées, fragments et lettres de Blaise Pascal,* Paris, 1897.
12. A. Huxley. *The perennial philosophy.* London. 1946.

# 15. Mysticism

Whatever may be our opinion on the social value of the contemplative life, it is generally agreed that mysticism is a subject of study which should not be ignored by the psychologist of religion. William James, in his famous Gifford Lectures at the beginning of this century, led the way in this interest. The characteristic of mysticism which first attracts the attention of the psychologist is the fact that the mystic experiences alterations in consciousness which culminate in a state which he describes as that of Union. This is described by the theistic mystic as the experience of union with God. A similar state of consciousness may be experienced by a non-theistic mystic (e.g. a Buddhist) who will describe it in other terms. Both the theistic and the non-theistic mystic will agree on the importance of the experience which they regard as a genuine perception of an aspect of reality, although they may differ widely in any verbal account they give of what is perceived.

The importance of mysticism for religious psychology is that it provides the creative impulse in religious thought. The mystic accepts his experiences as a form of immediate knowing of divine realities, which tends to make him an innovator in religion: St Paul, Fox and Mohammed, all made drastic changes in the religious tradition which they had inherited. This does not mean that the mystic is necessarily in conflict with conservative religious authority; he may avoid this conflict by accepting the orthodox tradition as a criterion for the truth of his own mystical perceptions. There is, however, the possibility of tension between the mystic's private revelation and the orthodox tradition that he accepts. He may resolve it by regarding as of diabolical origin those of his own ostensibly mystical perceptions that conflict with orthodox religious teaching. There have been other mystics, such as the Spanish *Illuminati* of the early seventeenth century, who have not accepted this check of orthodoxy and have been condemned as heretics. Some Roman Catholic writers, as, for example, Mgr Knox, refer to these as 'false mystics'.[1] This implied distinction between 'true' and 'false' mysticism does not appear to be well-founded; it would seem more reasonable to regard them as essentially the same psychological condition differing from each other only in subjection to or independence of traditional orthodoxy.

The psychological student of the mystical life will want to include under the term 'mystic' not only Christian contemplatives of various degrees of orthodoxy as judged from the point of view of any particular Christian body, but also those who have trodden a parallel path in the religious traditions of Islam, of Hinduism, of Buddhism, etc. In examining the course that leads to the contemplative life we find two related types of activity which show a remarkable degree of parallelism within different religious traditions. These are: first, systems of mental exercises which have already been discussed in the chapter on meditation, and secondly a system of behaviour rules which we may call the *ascesis*. The characteristic of these behaviour rules is that they require a habitual refusal to carry out certain instinctive or customary actions and a habitual carrying out of actions which are painful in themselves or against which there is an instinctive repugnance. Thus Christian mystics have fasted and cut short their sleep as well as abstaining from sexual activity and ordinary social intercourse; some have practised more drastic austerities by denying themselves ordinary comfort or by scourging themselves. Such ascetic activities can be paralleled in other religions. Abú Sa'íd, the Muslim mystic, who shocked other Sufis by the richness of his feasts in his later life, spent many years in severe austerities. He fasted and used to recite the Koran while suspended head downwards.[2] Although it was regarded as one of the characteristics of the teaching of the Buddha that he rejected the extreme asceticism of the yogins of his time, the way of life he required of his followers would be regarded as very austere by any ordinary standards. The monastic brethren refrained from the eating of meat and all sexual activity; they were restricted to one meal a day and were forbidden to own anything. Their mental exercises were directed towards the same end as their behaviour abstentions. They were trained to think of the disgusting associations of food and drink and of their transformations in the body, so that they would cease to have any craving for food and drink. The Buddhist meditant also went to the cremation grounds and observed the loathsome nature of the dead bodies, and, considering living bodies in the same way, convinced himself that they too were repulsive.

The immediate aim of such exercises of body or mind was to produce a state of *indifference* in which there was neither craving for the pleasant nor aversion from the unpleasant. This condition is described in somewhat similar terms in different religions. Thus the Buddha spoke in his earliest recorded discourse of the 'noble truth of the cessation of pain: the cessation without remainder of craving, the abandonment, forsaking, release, non-attachment'.[3] The same idea is expressed in the Hindu *Bhagavad-Gita* where it speaks of the serene one who 'knows no disquiet in heat or in cold, in pain or pleasure, in honour or dishonour'.[4] In somewhat similar terms, Ignatius of Loyola said:

It is necessary that we should make ourselves indifferent to all created things, in all that is left to the liberty of our free-will, and is not forbidden; in such sort that we do not for our part wish for health more than sickness, for wealth more than poverty, for honour more than dishonour, for a long life more than a short one, and so in all other things; desiring and choosing only that which leads us more directly towards the end for which we were created.[5]

Self-love is perhaps the most crippling of the cravings from which the person on the contemplative path needs to be liberated. This is not destroyed by mere bodily austerities; indeed, these can minister to self-love if they are regarded as spiritual achievements. Yet the destruction of self-love is an important part of the ascetic path, as is also the destruction of the satisfaction felt in the esteem of other people which is one of the roots of self-love. At this stage, the ascetic accepts as disciplines or inflicts on himself events tending to lower his self-esteem or the esteem of his fellows for him. It may be said that he is now trying to destroy self-love as he was trying earlier to destroy object-love. A typical action of this stage is that of an Egyptian Father who, on approaching a town and seeing a crowd of people who had come out to do him honour, took off his clothes and went on naked so that people should laugh at him and call him a madman instead of esteeming him as a saint.[6] The ascesis of self-love would appear to be one of the constituents of what St John of the Cross referred to as the 'Night of the Spirit'.[7]

The states of consciousness that are characteristic of mysticism are the various forms of mystical prayer. Although names have been given (by St Teresa and other writers) to different stages of mystical prayer, it is also convenient to have a single name to include them all. A generally accepted term for this purpose is 'contemplation'. There is an unfortunate ambiguity in this term since it is also used for the condition of interior quietness which may be produced in meditational practice by the deliberate suppression of imagery and discursive thought. This state has been called 'acquired contemplation' in order to distinguish it from the 'infused contemplation' of mystical prayer. In both conditions there may be partial or complete disappearance of imagery and discursive thought, although in infused contemplation this disappearance is not aimed at directly. Thinking on this subject might be clearer if the word 'contemplation' were reserved solely for the mystical states of consciousness, while those states of consciousness which result from the deliberate suppression of imagery and verbal thinking were called by some other name. There are, in fact, alternative names for these latter states. In Hindu thought they are referred to as states of 'one-pointedness'; a commonly used term in the Christian tradition is 'the prayer of simple regard'.

Infused contemplation is described by the mystics themselves in such terms as: 'the ineffable perception of God', 'the experimental knowledge of God's in-dwelling and presence within us', and 'the direct apprehension of God'. Such language does not seem to be meant to imply merely a state of effortless concentration whose object is the idea of the presence of God. That might be an adequate description of the prayer of simple regard but such terms as 'ineffable perception', 'experimental knowledge' and 'direct apprehension' would not be chosen to describe the experience of the prayer of simple regard. This does not mean that in infused contemplation the experience is necessarily clearer than in non-mystical prayerful states of consciousness. On the contrary, the passage into mystical prayer is often described in terms which show that it has appeared to the person experiencing it as a passage from clear thinking to a relatively confused perception. So it follows that the words 'darkness' and 'night' may be used of the experience of mystical prayer, while the anonymous author of a well-known fourteenth-century book on mystical prayer entitled his book *The cloud of unknowing*.

Another characteristic reported of mystical prayer is the limited extent to which it is under voluntary control. It appears that the non-mystical condition which has been called 'acquired contemplation' can be entered into or left at will. A state of infused contemplation, on the other hand, is liable to begin or end without any intention or expectation on the part of the person experiencing it. If a person experiencing infused contemplation wishes to emerge from this state because it is interfering with necessary activities, he may find himself unable to do so merely by directing his attention to other things. He has to make vigorous bodily movements or to walk up and down. If he is in the ecstatic stage of mystical prayer he will be unable to do even this, since the power of bodily movement may be completely suspended. Sadhu Sundar Singh has described the care he had to exercise lest he should 'slip into' ecstasy while he was working in cities and wished to be able to address public meetings.[8]

It is not only at an advanced stage of prayer that there occur involuntary alterations of consciousness which those experiencing them are inclined to regard as direct perceptions of spiritual reality. In Chapter 5 examples have already been quoted, such as the man on a country walk who reported: 'The wonderful beauty filled me with excitement and delight. And then suddenly, through all that I saw, there came the very glory of God.' Such experiences have been called 'nature mysticism' and they may or may not be preludes to later experiences of infused contemplation. Their interpretation depends on the previous belief system of the person experiencing them and they may not always be interpreted theistically. Zaehner calls such experiences 'pan-en-henic'.[9] He regards them not as true mystical experiences but as belonging to the same class as the alterations of consciousness which may occur in mania or as the result of taking psychedelic drugs. Whether such experiences are called mystical depends perhaps more on the criteria by which one defines mysticism than on any characteristic of the experience itself. Both the pan-en-henic experience and the infused contemplation of the religious mystic have as their most prominent component the sense that they give direct perception of spiritual realities. No doubt they differ in other respects.

There have been many different systems of classification of mystical states. Some writers have made a simple three-fold division into the way of 'purgation', of 'illumination', and of 'union'. St John of the Cross spoke of two dark nights of the soul, the 'night of sense' and the 'night of the spirit'.[7] St Teresa described four stages of mystical prayer: the 'prayer of quiet', the 'prayer of union', 'ecstasy', and the 'spiritual marriage', distinguished by various introspective and behavioural criteria.[12] This classification has been very commonly followed by modern Roman Catholic writers on prayer.

The prayer of quiet is the first stage of infused contemplation. It occurs usually, but not always, to someone whose practice of meditation has already led to the state of consciousness described as acquired contemplation. It is reported to come at first for only a few seconds, but later it may continue for many hours, even through a period of physical activity. The power of making bodily movements is not lost although movement usually brings the state to an end. The prayer of quiet differs from later stages of mystical prayer principally in the extent to which the state of contemplation is accompanied by distracting images and thoughts. In Teresa's own words:

> the will, entirely united to God, is much disturbed by the tumult of the thoughts: no notice, however, should be taken of them, or they would cause a loss of a great part of the favour the soul is enjoying. Let the spirit ignore these distractions and abandon itself in the arms of divine love.

The next stage distinguished by St Teresa is the *prayer of union* which would seem to be a deepened condition of the same state of consciousness as that of the prayer of quiet but without disturbance by distracting thoughts. In her own words:

> In the prayer of union the soul is asleep, fast asleep, as regards the world and itself: in fact, during the short time this state lasts it is deprived of all feeling whatever, being unable to think on any subject, even if it wished. No effort is needed here to suspend the thoughts: if the soul can love – it knows not how, nor whom it loves, nor what it desires.

Another state of consciousness found in mystical prayer is that of *ecstasy* in which there is loss of ordinary perceptual experience and of the power to make bodily movements. The cataleptic condition of the ecstatic's body has excited the wonder of those around and has contributed to the considerable religious interest in the phenomena of ecstasy. St Teresa says of ecstasy:

> Sometimes the person is at once deprived of all the senses, the hands and body becoming as cold as if the soul had fled; occasionally no breathing can be detected ... This supreme state of ecstasy never lasts long, but although it ceases, it leaves the will so inebriated, and the mind so transported out of itself that for a day, or sometimes for several days, such a person is incapable of attending to anything but what excites the will to the love of God.

A more recent introspective account of ecstasy has been given by the Sadhu Sundar Singh.[8] 'No words are spoken', he reported, 'but I see all pictured; in a moment problems are solved, easily and with pleasure, and with no burden to my brain.' He found that ecstasy was liable to occur after about twenty minutes of prayer and meditation. Then, sometimes for several hours, he lost all perception of the external world and had no sense of the lapse of time. He reported that once, during an ecstasy, he was stung all over with hornets, but he had felt nothing. When St Teresa ranks ecstasy as a stage of mystical prayer above that of the prayer of union, this seems to imply a valuation of ecstasy higher than that accorded to it by other writers on mystical prayer. St John of the Cross, on the other hand, seems to regard ecstasy as belonging rather to the imperfections of an early stage of mystical prayer. He speaks of 'ecstasies, raptures, and dislocation of the bones which always happen when these communications are not purely spiritual'.[7]

In its behavioural aspect, the ecstasy of the Christian mystics appears to be the same as the *samadhi* of the holy men of Hinduism. It may not be right to say that Christian ecstasy and Hindu samadhi are identical; they must differ in their cognitive content since they are rooted in different systems of ideas. Examples of descriptions of samadhi are to be found in the record of the life of Sri Ramakrishna who lived during the middle part of the nineteenth century and followed the way of 'bhakti-yoga', that of loving devotion. When talking to his surrounding disciples about the love of God, he is reported frequently to have entered into samadhi:

> While singing, the Master went into samadhi. He was seated on the bench, facing west, the palms of his hands joined together, his body erect and motionless. Everybody watched him expectantly ... After a time Sri Ramakrishna showed signs of regaining the normal state. He drew a deep breath and said with a smile: The

means of realising God are ecstasy of love and devotion – that is, one must love God.[10]

The experience of samadhi was described from the inside by Ramakrishna himself in the following words: 'Oh what a state of mind I passed through! When I first had that experience, I could not perceive the coming and going of day or night. People said I was insane. What else could they say? They made me marry. I was then in a state of God-intoxication.'

It is in the stage of ecstasy that certain other of the more striking events of mysticism are particularly liable to occur. These include such subjective events as visions and locutions and the occurrence of observable paranormal events among which extra-sensory perception, paranormal cures of diseases and injuries, and levitations have been reported. Neither of these types of event is peculiar to the stage of ecstasy but both seem to be more commonly associated with it. Both play a large part in the accounts given of the mystics by their biographers. This simple enthusiasm for the marvellous has not, however, generally been shared by the mystics themselves. Visions and locutions may be accepted as gifts from the spiritual world but they are considered as methods of illumination to be dangerously open to the possibility of deception. Some may be considered to be not gifts of God but deceptions from the devil. This distrust is paralleled in the distrust of the paranormal powers which are reported to occur in the spiritual development of the yogin.[11]

St Teresa classified visions and locutions into three groups: *exterior* in which what is seen or heard seems to the percipient to belong to the outside world, *imaginal* (or *imaginary*) in which what is seen or heard has a perceptual quality but is not mistaken for an event of the outside world, and *intellectual* visions and locutions which have no perceptual character but an inner feeling of a presence or a communication.[12] The distinction between exterior and imaginal visions would seem to be that commonly made in psychology between *hallucinations* and *pseudo-hallucinations*. In both cases, there is a perceptual experience which does not correspond to any external object, but the person experiencing a hallucination thinks that something is there in external fact, whereas the person experiencing a pseudo-hallucination knows that it is not so. The use of the term 'hallucination' for a religious vision does not prejudge the question of whether it has a spiritual cause; it is called a hallucination because it has no external material cause. St Teresa's evaluation of these three gives the first rank to the *intellectual* visions and locutions which she considered to be highly trustworthy. She considered that *imaginal* visions were less so, while she regarded *exterior* visions with considerable suspicion since she thought that, although they might be due to divine agency, they might alternatively be counterfeited by the devil.

Such hallucinatory experiences of vision and hearing are not uncommon in some forms of mental disorder. They are relatively uncommon amongst sane people except for hypnagogic hallucinations which occur in the state between sleeping and waking. It is true that a statistical enquiry suggested that about one in five persons experienced a hallucination at some time of their lives but these were usually isolated experiences.[13] The relative commonness of such experiences as an element of the religious life suggests that religious visions and locutions form a class by themselves. Certainly those experiencing them commonly show no insanity as judged by other criteria.

It is interesting to ask whether the visions and locutions experienced in ecstasy and related states are veridical in the sense that they convey true information not previously known to the percipient. I know of no investigation specifically directed towards answering this question, but there are a number of observations which show that frequently the contents of religious visions are not veridical, but rather are determined by current opinions of the religious group to which the percipient belongs. Thurston notes, for example, that Theresa Neumann had visions of the later history of St Mary Magdalen, including her passage in a ship without sails and rudder and the cave in which she died.[14] Both are elements in the legend of Mary Magdalen but are regarded by scholars as altogether unhistorical. Similarly many ecstatics have had visions of the crucifixion which correspond to the usual representation in works of art but which modern opinion rejects as unlikely to correspond to the actual facts of a crucifixion: e.g. the wounds on the palms of the hands, and the carrying by Jesus of the upright part of the cross (which is now commonly supposed to have been a fixture at the place of crucifixion).

The alterations of consciousness found in the prayer of quiet and more intensely in ecstasy were not, in St Teresa's opinion, the end of the road of the spiritual development found in mysticism. She describes also a later stage, of *spiritual marriage,* in which the previous trance conditions virtually disappear as do also the exterior and imaginal visions and locutions found in ecstasy. The state of contemplation, previously intermittent, is reported to become permanent at this stage, which is also characterised by a marked impulsion towards active work. In St Teresa's words: 'when the soul arrives at this stage it does not go into ecstasies except perhaps on rare occasions ... the sorrow and distress which such souls felt because they could not die and enjoy our Lord's presence are now exchanged for as fervent a desire of serving Him, of causing Him to be praised, and of helping others to the utmost of their power'.

In the terms of Jung's psychology, one would be inclined to describe this condition as one of extroversion experienced as God-directed which succeeds the earlier phase of God-centred introversion. One may wonder whether this is an invariable course of mystical development or whether it was merely an autobiographical detail of the spiritual development of St Teresa. Most likely there is something of both elements in it. Other mystics have been predominantly extroverted during the whole of their mystical lives. St Catherine of Genoa, for example, does not seem to have passed through an introverted phase since she spent her life in active work in a hospital at Genoa.[15] It seems likely that there are individual differences in the personality patterns of different mystics and that the change from an introverted to an extroverted kind of religious activity is characteristic of only some of them. It is, however, found in others besides St Teresa. Mme Guyon described her *apostolic state* which seems to have been parallel to the spiritual marriage of St Teresa. A similar condition is reported in Islamic mysticism for which the Sufis use the expression: 'Abiding after passing away'.[2] Abú Sa'íd, for example, at first practised austerities and experienced a passing away from self which seems to have been a state parallel to contemplation. This occurred at intervals till his illumination became permanent. After this time, he was active and gave up his previous austerities so far that his enemies accused him of self-indulgence. Abú Sa'íd described this active phase in language reminiscent of St Teresa's account of the spiritual marriage: 'The true saint goes in and out amongst the people and eats and sleeps with them and buys and sells in the market and marries and takes part in social intercourse, and never forgets God for a single moment.'

One of the aspects of mysticism which has aroused considerable discussion is that of the relationship of some of its phenomena to the symptoms of mental disorder. Dr Janet has published a study of a patient at the mental hospital of Salpêtrière whom he described as an ecstatic.[16] Over a period of twenty years, she showed a regular series of successive states with a religious content. These were: a state of *temptation*, one of *dryness*, one of *torture* (with fear of hell) and one of *consolations* (with ecstatic joy). This case would seem to differ from that of the typical religious mystics in the absence of any development over this period; there seems to have been simply a repeated sequence of emotional states. It seems that this was a case of a mental disorder utilising religious ideas rather than one of a religious development showing pathological symptoms.

More clear evidence of the connection between mysticism and mental disorder is provided by the mystics who showed evidence of hysteria and of pathological symptoms connected with high suggestibility. Baron von Hügel, for example, shows how the symptoms of hysteria detailed by Pierre Janet can be parallelled in the life of St Catherine of Genoa, particularly in her last illness. Anaesthesia, with loss of skin sensitivity over parts of the body, is a typical hysterical symptom; it is recorded of St Catherine that she would 'press thorny rose-twigs in both her hands, and this without any pain.'[16] Also she showed a typical hysterical exaggerated affective reaction to contact. At one time, 'she was so sensitive, that is was impossible to touch her very clothes or the bedstead, or a single hair on her head, because in such case she would cry out as though she had been grievously wounded'. There was a similar excessive reaction to certain colours; it is recorded that she could not bear the continued presence in her room of her physician in his red robes. These and other symptoms shown by St Catherine of Genoa suggest strongly that she did in fact suffer from hysteria.

This might in itself be of no more significance to the theory of mysticism than the fact that Ramakrishna died of cancer. That the association between hysteria and mysticism is not a purely accidental one is shown, however, by the frequency of other symptoms of heightened suggestibility shown by some ecstatics. In particular, there is the phenomenon of the stigmata which first appeared as marks of the wounds of Christ on the body of St Francis of Assisi in the thirteenth century and have since been reported in hundreds of ecstatic individuals up to the present time. Of these reported hundreds, Fr Thurston considers that about fifty are well attested.[14] This would seem to be a typical phenomenon of auto-suggestion in which the idea of the wounds of Jesus, strongly entertained by an individual of the highly suggestible hysterical type, is realised as actual bodily marks from which at times blood may be seen to flow. That the appearance of stigmata is essentially a phenomenon of suggestion is strongly indicated by the fact that it was virtually unknown before the publicity given to the case of St Francis when it became not infrequent, and also by the fact (pointed out by Thurston) that those who developed stigmata often had other symptoms of hysterical illness in their lives.

One might be led from these facts to surmise that mysticism is merely hysteria as misunderstood at a time when men were inclined too readily to accept supernatural explanations of natural phenomena. There seems to be sufficient reason for supposing that this view would be mistaken. It appears that some kinds of mysticism are closely related to hysteria but this does not seem to be true of all kinds of mysticism; hysteria is said by Jung to be a disorder of the extroverted personality, so it would not be reasonable to expect it to accompany mysticism of the more typical introverted kind. A proper under-standing of mysticism requires recognition of its being a phase of spiritual development. If some of its psycho-physical accompaniments are those of a secular mental disorder, this is not sufficient reason for concluding that the spiritual factor in it is unreal. Spiritual stresses in the mystic may produce the same sort of psycho-physical results as are produced by the non-religious stresses of other individuals.

Although much of the literature of Christian mysticism was written many centuries ago, it would be a mistake to think of mysticism as a purely mediaeval phenomenon. Mystics are also to be found at the present time. Some of these find their most natural home within the walls of contemplative religious communities; some of them live in the world. Such individuals may be looked at askance by more conventionally religious individuals. These may judge mysticism to be a degenerate form of religion which directs its interests away from the social problems that are regarded as the chief concern of the right-minded Christian. This judgment may not seem to be altogether just if one considers how large a part has been played in the lives of at least some mystics by love-directed activity in the world.

There is, however, a real difference in emphasis between the contemplative and the world-centred Christian in their relative valuation of spiritual experience and of works of active charity. It may be urged, in defence of the mystics, that they make a distinctive contribution to creative thought in religion and to the awareness that there may be a spiritual world to which we must adjust ourselves as well as to this world of space and time. The mystic himself would, no doubt, feel that he needed no such defence. If man's highest activity is to love God, it is reasonable to regard mysticism as being of value as an end in itself, and not merely because of any usefulness it may have in this world.

REFERENCES

1. R. A. Knox, *Enthusiasm*, Oxford, 1950.
2. R. A. Nicholson, *Studies in Islamic mysticism*, Cambridge, 1921.
3. M. Muller (Ed.), 'Discourse on the foundation of the kingdom of righteousness', *Sacred books of the East*, XI, Oxford, 1881.
4. Swami Prabhavananda and C. Isherwood (Translators), *The song of God (Bhagavad-Gita)*, London, 1947.
5. W. H. Longridge, *The spiritual exercises of Saint Ignatius of Loyola*, London, 1919.
6. E. A. T. W. Budge, *The paradise or garden of the Holy Fathers*, London 1907.
7. St John of the Cross, *The dark night of the soul* (Eng. trans.), London, 1916.
8. B. H. Streeter and A. J. Appasamy, *The Sadhu*, London, 1921.
9. R. C. Zaehner, *Mysticism sacred and profane*, Oxford, 1957.
10. Swami Nikhilananda (Trans.), *The gospel of Sri Ramakrishna*, Madras, 1944.
11. Patanjali, 'Yoga Sutras', *Harvard Oriental Series*, Cambridge (Mass.), 1914.
12. St Teresa, *The interior castle* (Eng. trans.), London, 1912.
13. H. Sidgwick, *et al.*, 'Report on the census of hallucinations', *Proceedings of the Society for Psychical Research*, X, 1894, pp. 25–422.
14. H. Thurston, *The physical phenomena of mysticism*, London, 1952.
15. F. von Hügel, *The mystical element of religion*, London, 1908.
16. P. Janet, *De l'angoise à l'extase*, Paris, 1927 and 1928.

# 16. Practical problems of religious diversity

The primary aim of applying the psychological method of study to the problems of religion is to promote understanding of religion. Its aim is not to create or to destroy religious belief, nor is it concerned primarily to change people's attitudes towards religions, although such changes in attitude may be secondary consequences of the study. An attitude that may well be changed is the one adopted towards other religions and towards variations within one's own religious tradition. These are commonly referred to as attitudes of 'tolerance' and 'intolerance'. The terms cover a considerable range of possible behaviours towards deviating individuals or towards members of other groups. Members of a religious group may be intolerant of deviations from the norm of belief or practice within that group, and the penalty for the deviating individual has ranged from exclusion from the group to death by burning. A different intolerance is shown towards members of other religions who may be regarded as worshippers of unreal or evil gods. The behaviour resulting from this intolerance has ranged from making war against such worshippers to engaging in missionary activity to convert them to the true religion.

It is part of the business of the psychology of religion to study objectively these attitudes of tolerance and intolerance and to consider the possibility and desirability of modifying them. As terms for the purpose of objective study, 'tolerance' and 'intolerance' are open to the objection that in common speech they are inclined to carry emotional meanings of approval and disapproval; we think of tolerance as a good thing and of intolerance as a bad thing. As descriptive terms in social psychology they must be used without this emotional implication, as descriptions rather than evaluations. Intolerance of new ideas or of alien cults is a social fact whose consequences may be judged good or bad. It may lead to such evils as persecutions or holy wars; it may serve useful ends such as keeping a superior tradition free from the intrusion of corrupting influences. In particular contexts the effect of these attitudes may be good or bad, and we may ask whether we should wish to modify them in one direction or the other.

One of the situations in which different religious traditions show greater or lesser degrees of tolerance is in their willingness to assimilate elements of belief and practice from other religions.

Judaism, Islam and Christianity are, for example, much less tolerant of such assimilation than are Hinduism and Buddhism. The many gods worshipped in India have been a result of free assimilation of the gods of people with whom they came in cultural contact. While Buddhism rejects the Hindu gods as objects of worship, this rejection does not prevent a shrine of a Hindu god being found in a Buddhist temple, or the ordinary Buddhist worshipper from offering petitionary prayer to the Hindu god. Though Buddhism has assimilated alien elements less freely than Hinduism, we find in the Lamaism of Tibet a typical end-result of free assimilation with an elaborate form of ritual and worship which seems far removed from primitive Buddhism.[1]

Similar assimilation did also take place to a lesser degree in Judaism, and afterwards in Christianity, but against strong resistance. Assimilation of alien cults was tolerated by such Jewish kings as Solomon and Ahab but against such tendencies the prophets waged a war which was on the whole successful. The massacre of the priests of Baal by Elijah was a typical demonstration of intolerance towards other religions. One can imagine an Indian sage approaching Elijah with the suggestion that Baal and Jehovah might be regarded as alternative symbols of the One God for whom no symbol is adequate. It cannot be doubted that Elijah would have rejected this point of view as fiercely as he rejected the worship of Baal.

Intolerance and tolerance are psychological attitudes determining behaviour; they are also reflected in ways of religious thinking and these are to some extent modifiable. The typical pattern of the less tolerant type of religious thinking treats the objects of worship in that religion as the only true God, while the gods worshipped in other religions are regarded either as unrealities or as real but evil beings. The alternative way of thinking, more favourable to tolerance, considers that there is one true God (or one true system of gods) to whom different religions have given different names and about whom different religions have different ideas. This way of thinking clearly does not imply that none of these systems of ideas are erroneous; it is indeed consistent with it to hold that all the systems of ideas about God held by the religions are in error. Nor does it entail an unlimited tolerance, but it does allow a larger tolerance of other religions than does the belief in one true God contrasted with a number of other false (non-existent or evil) gods.

A typical statement of this attitude is to be found in the *Bhagavad-Gita;* 'Even those who worship other deities, and sacrifice to them with faith in their hearts, are really worshipping me, though with a mistaken approach.'[2] Although such an idea comes more naturally to the highly tolerant tradition of Hinduism than to that of Christianity, similar lines of thought are now to be found amongst those belonging to the Christian tradition. Simone Weil, for example, has suggested that every time a man has, with a pure heart, called upon Osiris,

Dionysus, Krishna, Buddha, the Tao, etc., the son of God has answered him by sending the Holy Spirit.[3] She does not, however, mean to imply indefinitely wide toleration since she has said elsewhere that, though all religions pronounce the name of God in their particular language, all religions are not equally suitable for the recitation of the name of the Lord.[4]

It must of course be remembered that some of the consequences of an attitude of religious intolerance would ordinarily be regarded as desirable. Amongst these is the keeping of a superior religious tradition free from degenerative change. That, no doubt, was what Elijah and the Maccabees felt that they were doing. They did not want to see the worship of the One God corrupted by the assimilation of the deities of the Canaanite and other surrounding nations. They did not want Judaism to develop in the way that Hinduism has in fact developed.

Hinduism provides an example of the development of the tendency to tolerant assimilation against which the prophets were struggling. Alien elements of belief and practice have been freely taken in by the Hindu system while diversities within its own system have also been tolerated. Consequently, the beliefs of Hinduism range from polytheism through monotheism to atheism, and its religious practices vary from sacrificial rituals to meditations of ascetics who may regard these rites as spiritually useless and the gods worshipped as fanciful presentations of the One who cannot be comprehended. Yet Hinduism remains a strongly unified religion with its members united, not by identity of religious doctrine, but by the acceptance of a common priesthood.

Looked at from the point of view of a religious tradition intolerant of such diversity, Hinduism may be judged in Sir Charles Eliot's phrase to be 'a jungle and not a building'.[5] It was to prevent Judaism, and afterwards Christianity, from developing into such a jungle that the enforcers of uniformity from Elijah to Torquemada waged their war against the intrusion of alien religious elements and deviations from the one right system of beliefs. This war entailed much cruelty. Those waging it burnt at the stake devout unorthodox thinkers who might in India have become ascetics meditating in a temple court. It also produced a disastrous deviation of aim. While ecclesiastical courts were deciding whether a teacher had strayed from the proper doctrine of the Incarnation, they were in danger of losing sight themselves of the central teaching by Jesus Christ of the duty of love. In addition, it is an obvious fact of social psychological history that the fight was not successful; it no doubt prevented Judaism and Christianity from changing as much as they might have done, but both did change in the course of their history and both changed in part by absorbing elements of other religions.

One of the changes that is now taking place in modern Christianity is a growing doubt of the value to religion of attitudes of intolerance. This is partly a reaction against the cruelties of intolerance in the past; we now regard it as unreasonable and wicked to have burned Anne Askew in the sixteenth century for denying the doctrine of transubstantiation and as no less unreasonable and wicked to have burned Joan Bocher in the reign of Edward VI for holding that Jesus did not take flesh of the Virgin Mary but passed through her body as water through a pipe. We can also no longer accept the theory lying behind the more extensive cruelties of the Crusaders against the infidels who regarded Mohammed as the prophet of God. It is also increasingly recognised that this was not an effective way of securing religious uniformity. Diversities of belief and practice developed in the Christian Church in spite of the persecutions and religious wars; in fact, persecutions may have served to increase diversities of doctrine while religious wars may often have helped the assimilation of elements from other religions when those taking part in them made social contacts with their enemies and had the opportunity to absorb some of their religious attitudes.

There are two important practical problems of religious toleration: that of toleration of diversities within one's own religious body and that of toleration of other religions. The first of these seems to be nearer solution than the second. Within the Christian tradition, it is generally agreed that a greater tolerance of diversity is desirable and many factors at the present day are tending to increase it. Religious people have begun to take a more objective attitude towards their differences; the psychological study of religion may provide one of the means of increasing this more objective attitude. The ecumenical movement and various unions achieved and proposed between Christian churches are evidence at the behavioural level of this increased tendency. It is true that not all movements towards religious unity accept the ideal of tolerance of diversity; some retain the hope that unity will come by the disappearance of diversity. There was, for example, a statement by an evangelical conference in Oxford in 1963 which emphasised the importance of the reunion of the Church of England with Free Churchmen and Roman Catholics, but went on to say: 'Such reunion requires as its basis full and uncompromising acceptance of the doctrinal principles set forth in the 39 Articles.' The likelihood of reunion, by full and uncompromising acceptance by others of one's own position is remote. Tolerance of diversity seems a more hopeful road to unity; reduction of diversity may follow later as a result of unity.

The idea that uniformity of belief is not a necessary condition for the organic unity of a social body is familiar outside the field of religion. The unity of a scientific society is the result of all its members having a common aim; it is neither expected nor desired that they should all have the same beliefs. This does not mean that the truth of the beliefs held by members is regarded as unimportant; the putting forward of a novel and generally unaccepted opinion would not, however, be regarded as a ground for exclusion from the society. Part of the function of the scientific society is to bring into the open such diversity of opinion, not because diversity is welcomed for its own sake, but in the hope that its free discussion will lead to fuller understanding of what is the right side in the matter under dispute.

It has already been mentioned that Hinduism has an attitude towards diversity of belief and practice which is very different from that inherited by Christianity from Judaism. Devotees may worship Vishnu, Siva, Kali or other gods by various rites in temples which may also accommodate contemplative sages to whom it appears that all these gods are imperfect representations of the one God and that the rites offered to them are useless since liberation can come only by that understanding which is the fruit of meditation. These differences in valuation of rites and beliefs do not, however, preclude an attitude of mutual tolerance between the sage and the worshippers. The worshippers do not want to burn the sage as a heretic but rather tend to honour him as a holy man. Nor does the sage regard it as his duty to discourage the worshippers from their rites. He is inclined rather to regard these as suitable religious activities at the stage of religious development attained by those taking part in them. He does, however, consider that this stage would have to be transcended for the achievement of liberation. This attitude of tolerance on the part of the sage towards what he regards as primitive religious rites and beliefs has been expressed by one of the exponents of the monistic *advaita* system: 'Let people quote the Scriptures and sacrifice to the gods, let them perform rituals and worship the deities, but there is no liberation without the realisation of one's identity with the Atman.'[6] The problem of mutual toleration between the meditating sage and the worshippers of the many forms of deities was also discussed by Sri Ramakrishna. He was a priest of the mother goddess Kali but had also achieved the goal of meditation by the *advaita* method in which the meditant rejects and passes beyond all the forms of God. He asked one of his disciples whether he believed in God with form or without form. When he received the reply that the disciple thought of God as formless, Ramakrishna said: 'that is quite all right. But never for a moment think that this alone is true and all else false. Remember that God with form is just as true as God without form'.[7]

The terms 'God with form' and 'God without form' belong to Hindu thought; the underlying contrast imposes a problem for other religions. In Christianity too there is a difference between those whose ideas about the spiritual world are definite and concrete and those whose religious ideas are more abstract. It may be popularly verbalised as the difference between those who do and those who do not believe in 'A benevolent old man in the sky'. With respect to this difference too one may consider that each group may misjudge the other. The second group may be judged by the first to have lost their religious faith and to be part-way on the road to atheism while the first group may be judged by the second to have religious ideas too primitive to be of any spiritual value. There is also in Christianity a place for the view that the worship of God with and without form may both be valid roads to the religious end.

The toleration by Hindu sages of wide diversity of religious practices amongst the multitude may go so far that they refuse to join in the usual condemnation by educated Hindus of the primitive idolatry found amongst many of the Indian people. When, for example, it was suggested to Ramakrishna that one should persuade people not to worship a clay image as God, he replied: 'Suppose there is an error in worshipping the clay image; doesn't God know that through it He alone is being invoked? He will be pleased with that very worship. Why should you get a headache over it?'[7] Similarly, Vinoba Bhave, in his addresses in prison, said:

> the Lord who pervades this vast universe is present in His fullness in the little image, in the grain of sand ... This is the meaning behind image-worship. Many people have opposed image-worship. Foreigners, and even thinkers of our own country, have found fault with it. But the more I think of it, the more I realise its beauty ... Image-worship is the *vidya,* the art, of experiencing the whole universe in a little object.[8]

The degree of tolerance of diversity found in Hinduism is not likely to commend itself to Christian thinkers. The aim of maintaining a pure stream of teaching and practice is not likely to be abandoned to such an extent that the worship of idols is regarded as an acceptable Christian practice. But the example of Hinduism brings sharply to a focus the question of how much diversity can be tolerated within a religious body and opens our minds to the possibility that these limits have been set too narrowly in the past. It also makes clear the fact of social psychology that diversity of belief and practice is not incompatible with a strongly unified religious body.

Christian bodies of different communions are finding it more easy to adapt themselves to their own diversity than any of them find it to adapt themselves to non-Christian religious bodies. Yet there is now widespread doubt as to whether the traditional condemnation of these as worshippers of false gods is appropriate. We know more about alien religions than we did when such condemnation was a standard response, and we realise how much they have in common with Christianity. It is more widely realised that something may be lost in religious understanding by the refusal to share the insights of the saints and sages of non-Christian religions. There is the further point that the world-wide struggle against the forces of evil may be rendered less effective by the failure of the different religions to take part in it side by side.

There has obviously been much change in attitude amongst Christian bodies towards non-Christian religions. Thus a Declaration of the Second Vatican Council states: 'Upon the Muslims, too, the Church looks with esteem. They adore one God, living and enduring, merciful and all-powerful.'[9] It refers also to Hinduism as a system in which men 'contemplate the divine mystery and express it through an unspent fruitfulness of myths and through searching philosophical inquiry'. This is a marked change from the time when the Muslims were regarded as infidels against whom it was the duty of Christian men to wage merciless war, and the Hindus were considered to be heathen idolators and worshippers of false gods. It does not perhaps go so far as to imply that Christians have anything to learn from non-Christian religions, but even the idea that Christians should respect them and try to understand them is a radical departure from past ways of thinking.

Some individuals have gone further than this and tried to adapt elements from alien religious practices to the ends of Christian devotion. A French Benedictine monk has, for example, made use of the *asana* postures of Hatha Yoga and of the *pranayama* methods of breath control as adjuncts to Christian prayer.[10] This does not imply an assimilation of yogic ideas; the author rejects any idea of identification of the self with God and the expectation that techniques can in themselves effect a union with God. It is not for him a question of turning this form of Yoga into something Christian but of bringing the benefits that arise from yogic disciplines into the service of the contemplative Christian life. He reports that these exercises and the ascetic discipline of the Yoga, make it easier for the grace of Christ to flow in him. A further degree of assimilation of alien religious cults or modes of thinking is to be found in the development of religious groups starting from a Christian cultural setting which absorb beliefs and practices derived from an alien religion, generally from Buddhism or Hinduism or from both. The rise of Theosophy in the late nineteenth century is an outstanding example. The assimilation of alien religious ways of thinking is found in such books as A. Huxley's *The perennial philosophy* whose object is to present as a religious system, what is considered to be the common factor in all religions. Neither of these tendencies has at present more than a negligibly small effect on the attitudes of the Christian religious bodies.

Greater readiness to assimilate elements of other religions may be found in Hindu contemplatives. Ramakrishna, for example, is reported to have passed through periods of Muslim, Christian and Buddhist devotion each culminating with a vision of the founder of that religion.[11] His Christian phase started as a result of having the Bible read to him; this gave him the desire to realise the Christian ideal. Then as he was looking at a picture of Jesus in the arms of his mother:

> he felt as though the picture had become animated and that rays of light were emanating from the figures of Mary and Jesus, entering into him and altogether changing his mental outlook ... His reverence for the Hindu Gods and Goddesses was swept away by this tidal wave, and in their stead a deep regard for Christ and the Christian Church filled his heart, and opened to his eyes the vision of Christian devotees burning incense and candles before the figure of Jesus.

During three days, this Christian attitude prevailed and during these days he neglected the worship of the goddess Kali in the temple. Then he had a vision of an extraordinary looking person of serene aspect of whom he said: 'This is the Christ who poured out his heart's blood for the redemption of mankind and suffered agonies for its sake. It is none else than the Master-Yogin Jesus, the embodiment of Love!' This was not the beginning of a permanent attitude of rejecting the Hindu gods and accepting Jesus Christ. Sri Ramakrishna did not become a Christian convert; he continued his service as priest of the Kali temple at Dakshineswar. But as an individual he had assimilated a certain degree of Christianity into his religious system. He henceforth regarded Jesus Christ (as he did also the Buddha) as one of the incarnations of God.

What Ramakrishna did may be regarded as an experiment in the psychology of religion, not an experiment carried out to satisfy scientific curiosity but one to accomplish a spiritual end. Such an experiment would be difficult for the psychologist studying religion unless he accepted a religious point of view. It may be, however, that such experiments will in future be carried out in laboratories studying the phenomena of religion. Some boldness in following new experimental methods will be needed if the psychological study of religion is to approach closer to the central problems of religion.

Whether we are considering the possible degrees of tolerance of diversity amongst Christian communions or amongst different religions, there are similar problems concerning the theoretical justification of such tolerance. In neither case does tolerance imply acceptance of the proposition that all of the mutually tolerant systems are equally true, or that all can be regarded as different aspects of the same truth. Different religions and different branches of the same religion often make mutually exclusive assertions. Not all of these can be true; some at least must be meaningless or false. It is, therefore, not unreasonable for a person to hold that the statements made in his particular religion are more true than those of other religions. Whether this is so or not may be discussed by theologians; intolerance of other religious positions will only seem to be justified if an unreasonable amount of certainty is attached to the answer to this question. We know that an unreasonable degree of certainty does tend to be attached to religious propositions. Psychological study may serve a useful purpose in reducing this tendency to theological certainty, so making more easy the tolerance of diversity of belief both within religions and between religions. The religiously committed individual may then accept the proposition that all the religions are roads to God, even though he may also believe that his own road is a better one than others.

## REFERENCES

1. C. Bell, *The religion of Tibet*, Oxford, 1931.
2. Swami Prabhavananda, and C. Isherwood, (Translators), *The song of God (Bhagavad-Gita)*, London, 1947.
3. Simone Weil, *Letters to a Priest* (Eng. trans.), London, 1953.
4. Simone Weil, *Waiting on God* (Eng. trans.), London, 1951.
5. C. Eliot, *Hinduism and Buddhism*, London, 1921.
6. Swami Madhavananda, *Viveka-Chudamani of Sankaracharya*, Calcutta, 1952.
7. Swami Nikhilananda, (Trans.), *The gospel of Sri Ramakrishna*, Madras, 1944.
8. A. Vinoba Bhave, *Talks on the Gita*, London, 1960.
9. W. J. Abbott, (Ed.), *The documents of Vatican II*, London, 1966.
10. Dom J.-M. Déchanet, *Christian Yoga* (Eng. trans. of *La voie du silence*), London, 1960.
11. Swami Ghanananda, *Sri Ramakrishna: his unique message*, Mylapore, Madras, 1946.

# 17. The empirical argument for religious faith

It is not the purpose of the psychological study of religion to provide proofs for or against either the general religious proposition that there is a spiritual world or any of the particular statements of a religious system of belief. Men believe or disbelieve these statements for a variety of reasons. Some of these reasons have been considered in the course of our enquiry but we have not asked whether the reasons for these beliefs or disbeliefs were sound ones. Yet the question of whether or not the religious point of view is reasonable is one that we are bound to ask ourselves, even though the limitations of our method of enquiry may be such as to preclude us from finding a final answer by its means.

There are two questions that we may ask about the grounds for acceptance or rejection of religious belief. There is first the psychological question of the causes of such holding or rejection. Secondly, there is the more philosophical question of whether there are good reasons for supposing that a religious belief system is true or false. These are questions that must be kept separate. The use of the method of confident reiteration may be a powerful method of inducing belief but it provides no guarantee that the belief so induced is a true one. Conversely, if the ontological argument for the existence of God were logically sound, it would presumably remain psychologically incapable of inducing conviction.

In the earlier chapters of the present book we have been concerned with pyschological causes of religious belief and not with logical grounds for supposing religious beliefs to be true or false. In the present chapter we shall concern ourselves with a special aspect of the second question: whether the results of a psychological study of religion give us reasonable grounds for deciding whether any religious belief system is, at least to some extent, a true one. We are asking this question not as philosophers but as thinking people who have a real though non-professional interest in considering whether their beliefs are true or false. This is to suggest that there may be empirical grounds for holding or rejecting a religious faith, grounds derived neither from revelation nor from philosophy but from the study of how things are. This is the method used in science: belief in a heliocentric solar system, in a gravitational system that determines movements of bodies on this earth and of the planets round the sun, and in the evolution of living organisms, are all beliefs based empirically on the observation of facts. The question is whether the conception of a spiritual world provides a model which better fits the observed facts than do those theories which deny a spiritual world.

At the present time the influence of scientific thinking is such that we are all inclined to prefer empirical ways of justifying belief. These are not, however, the only ways in which men may come to hold a religious system of beliefs. I do not think the empiricist should even suppose that they provide the only rationally justifiable ground for belief: a religious belief system may well be accepted as a revelation or on the ground that it can be adequately defended by philosophical arguments. If it is accepted as revelation this may mean that it is believed to be true on the authority of some written scripture or some authoritative social body or on the authority of an intuitive conviction of the person himself. I do not think that, provided the supporting authority is internally consistent, acceptance of religious belief as revelation should be condemned as irrational, although there are obvious difficulties in the rational communication of its authority to anyone not accepting the revelation. From the point of view of the believer in a revelation, the authority is guaranteed by itself and no contradiction to it will be accepted, but the rational reply of the unbeliever is that he does not accept the authority and therefore does not accept the authority's guarantee of its own authenticity. Against this refusal, the defender of a self-guaranteeing authority (whether of a scripture or a church or a private revelation) does not seem to have any better response than that of repeated affirmation. In psychological fact, this can prove very effective in producing acceptance of the authority affirmed, however weak it may seem from a rational point of view.

Another alternative to the empirical method of evaluating the truth of religious belief is that of philosophical speculation. If it were possible to produce a completely water-tight argument for the existence of God, this would obviously provide a completely rational ground for religious belief. There have been many attempts in the past to produce such an argument, from the 'ontological argument' that existence is a necessary attribute of a perfect being, to the 'argument from design' that the design in the world proves the existence of a designer. All have been criticised and judged by competent philosophers to be faulty. The discussion may go on amongst philosophers, but obviously an argument about whose validity philosophers dispute cannot be a sufficient ground for rational conviction amongst non-philosophers. The psychological ineffectiveness of the traditional arguments for the existence of God has already been commented on. It may be that some religious people have a mistaken belief that the philosophical case for religious faith is stronger than it is, or a hope that a coercive argument for the existence of God will one day be found. Philosophers do not encourage this hope, and it is generally agreed that the search for conclusive philosophical proof of the grounds for religious faith is one that should be given up.

This is the situation in which one is led to ask whether there can be empirical evidence for or against religion: whether an examination of how things are can provide grounds for believing or disbelieving religious assertions. The part of this question that concerns the psychologist of religion is whether the study of religious behaviour and religious experience gives any grounds for religious belief or disbelief. This is only part of the question of the empirical basis of religious faith since the facts studied in the psychology of religion are only part of the study of how things are. There might also be a case for (or against) religious faith from the facts of biology, geology or atomic physics but with those parts of the problem we are not here concerned. It is necessary to accept the fact that no empirical argument can give absolute certainty. By empirical means we are limited to establishing what is likely to be true but without the hope of attaining certainty. So far as he relies on the empirical method, the religious believer must be content with the hope that he can establish a positive conclusion with a sufficient degree of probability to serve as a basis of his own faith. He cannot hope by this means to establish it with a degree of certainty that will carry conviction to the unbeliever.

William James in his *Will to believe* discussed the problem of whether it is reasonable to hold any form of religious belief if there can be no certain demonstration of its truth by philosophical argument and if empirically derived arguments can only establish probabilities and not certainties.[1] His contention was that this is reasonable. The situation is one in which we have what James called a 'living, forced, and momentous' option. It is a living option because both alternatives, the acceptance of religious belief and its rejection, are possible to us, forced because no attitude of leaving the question open is possible (we must behave either as if religious belief is true or as if it is not), momentous because it may be of unlimited importance which choice we make. If, at the same time, it is an option which cannot be decided on intellectual grounds, James pleads for the right of voluntary adoption of faith. He said:

> Our passional natures not only lawfully may, but must, decide an option between propositions, whenever it is a genuine option that cannot by its nature be decided on intellectual grounds; for to say, under such circumstances, 'Do not decide, but leave the question open', is itself a passional decision – just like deciding yes or no – and is attended with the same risk of missing the truth.

James did not, of course, mean that we can believe anything, whether it be true or false, provided that we want strongly enough to believe it.

He was assuming that the belief in question was a *live* one, by which he meant that we thought that it might be true. If a belief is not, in this sense, a live one, no volitional effort can make it reasonable to accept it as true. For some people any form of religious faith based on belief in a spiritual world, does not appear to be a live alternative. For them, James's argument does not provide a gateway to religious acceptance. It can only become so when they become convinced that the spiritual interpretation of the world is a possible one, however alien it may be to their habits of thought.

James's argument does not take one far in the direction of the acceptance of religious belief. It may be regarded as a last ditch to which the religious believer can retreat from his opponent and from which he cannot be dislodged unless he can be persuaded that a spiritual interpretation of the universe is not possible. This could be convincingly demonstrated if his opponent could find a certain philosophical proof of the non-existence of God and of spiritual realities, but such a quest would seem to be as hopeless as that for a certain philosophical proof of their existence. Failing that, the opponent of religious faith must also establish probabilities by empirical evidence, or use the much more dubious appeal to current habits of thought, pointing out that a training in scientific thinking predisposes one to reject spiritual interpretations of the world. This is, no doubt, largely true although it is arguable that it is due to a defect in current scientific education and that the ideal training in scientific thinking would not affect the person subjected to it in quite this way. It might be hoped that it would predispose him to question his thought habits and to revise in the light of empirical evidence any opinions that were based on them.

A typical statement of the psychological case against religion is one made by Leuba in a discussion of the interpretation of the phenomena of mysticism:

> If there were extra-human sources of knowledge and superhuman sources of human power, their existence should, it seems, have become increasingly evident. Yet the converse is apparently true; the supernatural world of the savage has become a natural world to civilised man; the miraculous of yesterday is the explicable of today. In religious lives accessible to psychological investigation, nothing requiring the admission of superhuman influences has been found. There is nothing, for example, in the life of the great Spanish mystic whose celebrity is being renewed by contemporary psychologists, – not a desire, not a feeling, not a thought, not a vision, not an illumination, – that can seriously make us look to transcendent causes.[2]

The supporter of the religious point of view cannot contest the main point of this passage, that, if the feelings, visions, etc. of St

Teresa are entirely explicable in terms of a psychology which does not postulate transcendent causes, then the mere occurrence of these feelings and visions could supply no proof of transcendent causes; it might still be true that there was some feature of these feelings and visions that made us suspect transcendent causes and that might be regarded as indicating superhuman influences with some degree of probability. There is in fact an element of exaggeration in the suggestion that psychological investigation can give such complete understanding of the thoughts or feelings of anyone as to enable us to say with certainty that we fully understand their causes. Certainly psychology may give us fuller understanding of such things some time in the future. It will still not reveal transcendent causes because the theoretical system of psychology is one that at the outset refuses to refer to spiritual factors as it refuses also to refer to moral factors. The elimination of the moral and the spiritual in psychological explanation does not imply that these are not aspects of the reality studied, only that they are aspects of reality that are not admitted into the restricted language system of scientific psychology.

It should be noted that St Teresa herself did not consider that the mere occurrence of her visions and other religious experiences was a proof of their supernatural origin. When giving her reasons for believing that a particular form of ecstasy which she called 'the flight of the spirit' was neither an illusion nor the work of the devil, she said:

> neither the imagination nor the evil one could represent what leaves such peace, calm, and good fruits in the soul, and par-ticularly the following three graces of a very high order. The first of these is a perception of the greatness of God, which becomes clearer to us as we witness more of it. Secondly, we gain self-knowledge and humility as we see how creatures so base as ourselves in comparison with the Creator of such wonders, have dared to offend Him in the past or venture to gaze on Him now. The third grace is a contempt of all earthly things unless they are consecrated to the service of so great a God.[3]

This is to use a different criterion for the supernatural origin of a mystical experience than the mere occurrence of visions and feelings; it is also a criterion much more difficult to assess. The development of graces is not a matter which scientific psychology gives us any means of estimating. If the development of such graces is a proof of supernatural agency it may remain true (as Leuba said) that the psychologist can find nothing in the mystical experiences of St Teresa that makes it necessary for him to assume supernatural causes. It does not follow that there can be no grounds for believing in such supernatural causes; these may exist in directions not examined by the scientific psychologist.

It is also sometimes asserted that the supernatural view of the universe is a dead intellectual opinion which can be held by no reasonable person. This is justified by the contention that psychoanalysis can give an explanation of the origins of religious belief that does not assume any system of spiritual realities. Religion can be regarded as a socially tolerated form of neurosis in which the unconscious cravings of the subject are satisfied by an imaginary system which includes God and the spiritual world. That this explanation of the genesis of religious faith can be suggested is not, however, proof that it is true, still less that it is complete. It may be that one part of the reason why the frustrated individual turns to God and finds satisfaction in so turning is that there really is a God to whom he can turn. It has already been pointed out that some psychotherapists find the inculcation of religious motives an efficient part of their therapeutic method. The effectiveness of such a method is not strong proof that the supernatural world to which they turn is a reality and not merely a product of their imagination. It is, however, one of the pieces of evidence which must be considered as part of the empirical case for a religious point of view.

The arguments of William James that our passional natures can and must decide a living, forced and momentous option between alternative views, is a last ditch to which the defender of religious faith can be driven. He will wish to advance beyond it by considering grounds on which the religious view of a spiritual world is to be preferred to the denial of such a system of reality. He may feel that this religious view can be supported with a high degree of certainty by philosophical argument or by the acceptance of a revelation. As an alternative to these grounds for conviction or as a supplement to them he may adopt the empirical method of verifying his religious beliefs. He then asks whether the religious hypothesis of a spiritual world seems to fit the observed facts of this world and of his own inner experience.

The essential assumption of the empirical method of enquiry as to truth is that the system of thought which best explains observed facts is most likely to be true. If the religious system of ideas appears to explain one set of observations, that, let us say, of the experience of conflict between good and evil impulses in our own natures, this will be regarded as one piece of evidence that the religious system of ideas contains a true insight into the nature of reality. This would not, in itself, be a very strong ground for accepting a spiritual view of the universe; it might be that the facts of the moral conflict could have been explained in some alternative (non-spiritual) way.

The case becomes stronger if other observed facts of human life seem to indicate a spiritual explanation. There are, for example, the mystical experiences which seem to point to some system of spiritual realities. These too can carry no great weight to the non-mystic; they might be explained by him as products of illusion amongst individuals of unusual psycho-physical character. Yet they too form one strand in the empirical evidence for spiritual reality, even though their evidence would not be strongly convincing if it stood by itself.

The same may be considered to be true of the religious experiences of more ordinary people such as the experiences of spiritual immanence in Nature described in Chapter 5. These too may be explained as an illusory objectification of a euphoria which may merely be the result of a transient physiological condition. But they may also be explained as a true perception of a spiritual aspect of nature. If there are other grounds for believing in the reality of a spiritual world, such experiences must also be admitted as one element in the evidence for this reality.

One must also consider as part of the empirical case for religion the correlations between mental health and adjustment to spiritual reality noted by such psychotherapists as Jung, Maeder and Frankl which have been discussed in Chapter 10. If acceptance of a religious standpoint is a move towards mental health, this may be not because religious ideas are a health-giving delusional system, but because these ideas do indeed correspond to reality. If these asserted correlations are generally confirmed, they too supply a strand in the empirical case for the religious view of the universe.

There are also the facts of psychical research. As has been suggested in Chapter 11, these seem to fit in better with the conception of a spiritually based universe than with that of one limited to the material world. If any of the paranormal facts studied in psychical research are admitted as realities, and the evidence for some at least is very strong indeed, grave doubt is thrown on the materialist view of the universe; the spiritual interpretation of reality becomes more probable.

None of the lines of empirical evidence for the basic idea of religion, that of the reality of a spiritual world, would be a very strong ground by itself for accepting that reality. In conjunction they do make a strong case for it. It can reasonably be claimed that the spiritual way of looking at the universe makes more sense of many aspects of it than does the alternative view. It does not and cannot provide a certain demonstration that the religious point of view is the right one. So far as the religious man depends on the empirical method for justifying his faith, he has given up the quest for certainty. He may conclude on empirical grounds that the religious explanation of the universe is most likely to be true. He may feel the empirical argument provides sufficient reason for directing his life on the assumption that some form of religious faith is true. It cannot give him the certainty which could alone justify him in adopting an attitude of condemnation towards those who have accepted the opposite alternative in the choice between religious belief and unbelief.

REFERENCES

1. William James, *The will to believe, and other essays in popular philosophy*, London, 1897.
2. J. H. Leuba, *A psychological study of religion*, New York, 1912.
3. St Teresa, *The interior castle* (Eng. trans.), London, 1912.

# Index

ABBOTT, W. J., 140
ABU SA'ID, 122, 129
acts of devotion, 97
adolescent conversion, 59, 110
*advaita*, 11
aesthetic argument, the, 35
AKIRA KASAMATSU, 103
AL GHAZZALI, 115
anaesthesia, 129
anaesthetic experience, 4, 49
angels, 13
animism, 93
ANSELM, ST, 15, 66
*appanaka sutta*, 14
apparitions, 87
APPASAMY, A. J., 120, 131
AQUINAS, ST THOMAS, 117
Arahats, 61
ARCHER, W. G., 64
archetypes, 77
ARGYLE, M., 59, 63–4
arguments for the existence of God, 66, 142
ARISTOTLE, 10
asana positions, 97
asceticism, 61, 122
ASKEW, ANNE, 135
attitude, the religious, 11
AUGUSTINE, ST, 107–9
autonomic nervous system, 56
automatisms, 28, 50
auto-suggestion, 96

BALFOUR, JEAN, 89
BATEMAN, F., 89
beauty, 35
BEDE, 72
BEGBIE, H., 109, 120
behaviourism, 6, 9
BELL, C., 140
beneficence, 34
*Bhagavad-Gita,* 37, 122, 133
bhakti-yoga, 126
BHAVE, A. V., 137, 140
Bible, 14

BLOOD, COLONEL, 4
BOCHER, JOAN, 135
BONHOEFFER, D., 13, 14
BOOTH, WILLIAM, 111
breath control, 138
BROOKS, C. H., 103
BROWN, L. B., 70, 72, 94, 95
BROWNE, E. G., 64
BUDDHA, THE, 11, 12, 37, 42, 68, 85, 122
Buddhism, 10, 12, 13, 46, 61, 62, 69, 91, 98, 122, 133
BUDGE, E. A. T. W., 47, 132
BUNYAN, J., 42, 44, 47
BYLES, MARIE, 91, 94, 98, 103

CARLYLE, T., 57
CATHERINE OF GENOA, ST, 34, 118, 129
CAVAN, 59
CELLINI, B., 44, 47
ceremonial, 51
certainty, tendency to, 70
chastity, 60
Christianity, 11, 14, 133
    without religion, 13
*Cloud of unknowing,* 102, 124
COHEN, ELIE A., 64
collective unconscious, 77
communism, 10, 13
comparative religions, 14
confession, 45
consecration, 99
contemplation, 123
conversion, 41, 104–20
COUÉ, E., 96
cross-correspondences, 83
crowd psychology, 25
crucifixion, 128
CUMMINS, GERALDINE, 83, 89
CURÉ D'ARS, 85
CUTTEN, G. B., 55, 57

DALE, R. W., 38
dark nights of the soul, 125
DAVENPORT, F. M., 27, 29, 31

death, 62
deautomization, 102
DÉCHANET, J-M., 140
definition, 10–12
DEIKMAN, A. J., 102, 103
delinquency, 42, 47
depersonalisation, 64
deprivation of love, 3, 58
DESCARTES, R., 66
design, argument from, 32, 35, 67, 142
devil, the, 16
diversity of religions, viii, 132–40
dogma, 68
drug addiction, 41, 50
dualism, 16, 36, 40
DUCASSE, C. J., 92, 95

ecstasy, 126
education, religious, 5, 42, 94
EDWARDS, JONATHAN, 26
ELIJAH, 133
ELIOT, C., 134, 140
emancipation, 61
emotion, 56
emotional factor in religion, 48–57
ESDRAS, 87
eternal life, 84
Everlasting mercy, The, 107
evolution, 67
extra-sensory perception, 81
extroversion, 128

factor analysis, 19
fanaticism, 76
fasting, 61
FAUGÈRE, P., 120
fear, 26
FIELD, C., 120
FOX, GEORGE, 121
FRANCIS, ST, 38, 130
FRANKL, V. E., 78, 79, 147
FREUD, S., 9, 30, 61, 73–6, 79, 114
Friends, Society of, 69
FRYER, A. T., 31

GALTON, F., 93, 95
GHANANANDA, 140
GIDEON, 93
Gifford lectures, 2
glossalalia, 54
God, belief in, 4, 11
   love of, 42
GODIN, A., 5, 7, 93, 95
GOLDMAN, R., 5, 7
GORER, 60
GRAHAM, BILLY, 27

group suggestion, 24
guilt, sense of, 43–7
GURNEY, E., 89
GUYON, MME, 118, 129

habituation, 26
hallucination, 127
HARDY, SIR ALISTER, 7
HARDY, T., 37
HEGEL, G. W. F., 9
HEISENBERG, W., 9, 14
hell, 22, 26, 63
herd suggestion, 25
HIGHTOWER, P. T., 42, 47
HILLIARD, F., 47
Hinduism, 36, 60, 97, 122, 133, 134, 136, 138
holiness, 86
HOPKINS, G. M., 35, 38
HORNER, I. B., 72
humanism, 13
HUXLEY, A., 49, 57, 102, 104, 120, 138
hypnoidal state, 24
hypnotism, 21
hysteria, 27, 73, 129

idolatory, 137
IGNATIUS LOYOLA, ST, 98, 123
Illuminati, 121
illusion, 75
immortality, 4, 18, 63
indifference, 122
intellectual conversion, 106
   factor, 18, 65–72
intolerance, 69, 71, 105, 132
IRVING, E., 54
ISAACSON, C. S., 31, 120
ISHERWOOD, C., 38, 129, 140
Islam, 10, 13, 122, 133, 138

JAMES, WILLIAM, viii, 1–3, 5, 7, 49, 57, 59, 61,
   64, 91, 105, 110, 120, 121, 141, 148
JAMI, 61
JANET, P., 45, 47, 129, 133
JESUS CHRIST, 12, 84, 139
JEVON, F. B., 47
JOAD, C. E. M., 19, 107, 120
JOHN OF THE CROSS, ST, 60, 64, 123, 125, 131
Judaism, 10, 12, 13, 133
JULIAN, DAME, 30, 31, 40, 47
JUNG, C. G., 77–8, 79, 128, 130, 147

KANT, I., 66
KELSEY, M. T., 54, 55, 57
KNOX, R. A., 121, 131
KRETSCHMER, R. W., 103
KRISHNA, 60

Lamaism, 133
LE BON, G., 25, 31
LEIBNITZ, G. W., 66
LEUBA, J. H., 4, 7, 10, 11, 14, 144, 148
LONGRIDGE, W. H., 103, 129
love, 58

MADHAVANANDA, 140
MAEDER, A., 78, 79, 147
MARTHE, SOEUR, 7
MARY MAGDALEN, 128
MAY, L. C., 57
meditation, 7, 90, 96-8
meekness, 61
mental prayer, 90
mescalin, 49, 50, 102
MILLER, E., 57
mindfulness, 101
miracles, 84-7
MOHAMMED, 121
MOLINOS, M., 102, 103
moral argument, the, 40
 conflict, 16, 39, 47
MÜLLER, G., 91
MULLER, MAX, 89, 129
music, 51
MYERS, F. W. H., 10, 14, 89
mystical conversion, 116, 120
mysticism, 17, 34, 48, 121, 122, 123

Native American Church, 49
natural factor in religion, 32-8
 history of religion, 3
naturalism, 12, 80
nature mysticism, 124
needs, 17, 58-64
NEUMANN, THERESA, 128
NICHOLSON, R. A., 131
NIKHILANANDA, 89, 132, 140
NORTH, BROWNLOW, 22, 30
nuclear weapons, 27
NYANOPONIKA, THERA, 47

Oedipus complex, 74
old age, 59, 63
OLIPHANT, MARGARET, 57
one-pointedness, 97, 101, 124
ontological argument, 66, 142
oratory, 52
out-of-the-body experiences, 82

PAHNKE, W. H., 50, 57
PALEY, W., 32, 35, 38
Palm Sunday case, 83
pan-en-henic experience, 125
paranoia, 65

paranormal, the, 80
parapsychology, 80
pastoral work, 78
PASCAL, B., 116, 117-18
PATAÑJALI, 131
PATMORE, COVENTRY, 61, 64
PAUL, ST, 55, 104, 121
pentecostalism, 52, 53
persecution, religious, 69, 76
petitionary prayer, 35, 58, 90, 94
PFISTER, O., 76, 79
PIAGET, J., 93
PODMORE, F., 82
PRABHAVANANDA, 38, 131, 140
PRATT, J. B., 27, 31, 47
PRATT, J. G., 89
prayer, 90-4
presence of God, act of, 97
prophecy, 55, 82
providence, 34
pseudo-hallucination, 127
psilocybin, 50
psychedelic drugs, 4, 7, 50, 125
psychical research, viii, 80-8, 147
psychoanalysis, 2, 73
psycho-kinesis, 81
psychology, 8-9
psychoneurosis, 73-8
psychotherapy, 73-9

quiet, prayer of, 101, 125
quietism, 102

RAMAKRISHNA, 86, 126, 136, 137, 138
rationalisation, 17-18, 105
rationalism, 65
rattle-snakes, 53
reasoning, 17
relaxation of effort, 46
religion, definitions of, 9-14
repression, 73-105
revivals, 25-
RHINE, J. B., 89
RHINE, LOUISA E., 89
RHYS DAVIDS, T. W., 38, 64
RIBOT, T. A., 67, 72
RIVERS, W. H. R., 92, 94
Robert Elsmere, 107
ROBERTS, EVAN, 24, 28, 115
ROBINSON, J. A. T., 14
RULMAN MERSWIN, 116
RÜMKE, H. C., 76, 79

SALTMARSH, H. F., 89
samadhi, 126
sanctity, 1

SARIPUTTA, 46
scepticism, 70
seances, mediumistic, 83
self-hatred, 62
self-love, 123
self-naughting, 62
sentimentalism, 57
sermons, 97, 100
sex, 59, 114
Shaker religion, 29
SIDGWICK, H., 131
simple regard, prayer of, 101, 124
SLOTKIN, J. S., 57
SOAL, S. G., 89
social conversions, 105, 109
    factor, the, 20–30
Society for Psychical Research, 80
solitude, 61
sorcery, 86
spiritual marriage, 128
    world, 12
SPURGEON, C. H., 22–3, 28
STARBUCK, E. D., vii, 3, 7, 59, 64, 110, 113,
    120
statistical studies, vii
STEVENSON, I., 89
stigmata, 130
STREETER, B. H., 120, 131
stress, 26
subconscious incubation, 105, 110
sublimation, 74
sufism, 115
suggestibility, 21, 97
suggestion, 16, 20–30
SUNDAR SINGH, 109, 124, 126
survival after death, 62, 81
SUSO, HENRY, 119
Swearing Tom, 106
SWINBURNE, A., 33
SYMONDS, J. A., 49

TART, C. T., 7, 103
telepathy, 82, 83, 85–6

TERESA, ST, 123, 125, 127, 131, 144, 148
theistic religions, 13, 17, 33
Theosophy, 10, 138
THOREAU, H. D., 32, 38, 48
THURSTON, H., 89, 128, 129, 131
Todas, 92
TOKSVIG, SIGNE, 89
tolerance, 132, 139
TOLSTOY, L., 115
TOMIO HIRAI, 103
TORREY, R. A., 22, 31
totemism, 74
transference, 30
TROCHU, F., 89
TROTTER, W., 31, 65, 72
TYRRELL, G. N. M., 89

unconscious, the, 73
UNDERHILL, EVELYN, 120
unforgiveable sin, the, 44
union, prayer of, 125
Unitarians, 69

VAN ROEY, BERNADETTE, 93, 95
Vatican Council, 138
visions and locutions, 127
VON HÜGEL, F., 38, 129, 131

WARD, MARY A., 19
WEIL, SIMONE, 133, 140
Welsh revival, 28
WESLEY, JOHN, 28, 31, 116
WHITE, V., 121
WILKERSON, D., 47, 58, 64, 92, 94
will to believe, the, 143
wish-fulfillment, 41
WITTGENSTEIN, L., 10, 14

yoga, 97, 138

ZAEHNER, R. C., 125, 131
Zarathustrianism, 40
Zen, 100, 102